A Breath of Vyas

A Breath of Vyas

(*Vyasochchhvas*)

DILEEP JHAVERI

Translated from the original Gujarati
by Kamal Sanyal

Seagull
BOOKS

CALCUTTA 2006

Vyasochchhvas was first published in Gujarati
by Kshitij Sanshodhan Prakashan Kendra, Mumbai, 2002

This edition of the play in English translation
published by Seagull Books, 2006

ISBN 81 7046 485 4

Cover design by Sunandini Banerjee
using a drawing by Laxma Goud

Published in India by Naveen Kishore, Seagull Books Private Limited
26 Circus Avenue, Calcutta 700 017, India

Printed in India by Rockwel Offset
55 Mirza Ghalib Street, Calcutta 700 016

Exclusively distributed in South Asia by Foundation Books Pvt Ltd
Cambridge House, 4381/4 Ansari Road, Daryaganj, New Delhi 110 002
www.foundationbooksindia.com

Dedicated to

Professor K. Satchidanandan
who guided me to the adivasi originator
of the Mahabharata

Contents

Acknowledgements

My everlasting gratitude to Kamal Sanyal for translating the play and Anjum Katyal for encouraging its publication. I also thank Dharmesh Nehete, Lata Bagav, Madhura and Mugdha Gupte, Padma Aiyer for their help and especially Sarita Bose for typing out the play, and most of all to Raja Potdar. For the first Gujarati publication, *Etad* (Kshitij Sanshodhaṇ Prakashan Kendra).

I am grateful to Bharatiya Vidya Bhavan, Mumbai; Prithvi Theatre, Mumbai; Vyanjana, Rajkot for organizing readings, and also to Jagdeep Smart, Ms Jyoti Bhalaria, Madhu Manek, Niranjan Mehta, Rajendra Patel, Ramanik Agrawat, Sanju Wala and Shrish Panchal.

Preface

Why does the Mahabharata compel us to return to it time and again? However far we may fly, like birds we come back to the nesting place. The Mahabharata also is a place we start from.

In spite of being occupied by mega-dimensional polymorphic life, it has enough space for us to venture within and discover ourselves. Modestly titled a 'history' or 'itihasa' by its original author Krishna Dwaipayan Vyas, it is in reality eternal future and we find it relevant even today. Within it, we find the future foretold and the unpredictable anticipated.

It was relevant even a thousand years ago and also a part of the history of that time. The fact that it continued to be written over several centuries indicates its openness and foresight. Without discrimination it provided space to several writers of varying talents and ideologies. A vastly learned poet with a profound concern for human destiny and affairs would share the space equally with a folklorist entertaining the plebian. A skilful and masterly dramatist joined hands with a crafty pedant. Chroniclers of clan histories cohabited with canvassers of tourist spots. Experts in jurisprudence occupied a common platform with non-conventional visionaries.

Two thousand years ago the Mahabharata had anticipated the mass destruction that mankind was capable of. The scale of devastation that was dreamt of, the weapons that were imagined, the ecological disaster that was lamented, became a reality that we have witnessed in the last century.

Man's evil ingenuity finds its fullest, widest and wildest expression in the Mahabharata. Man's ambition to master the universe is ironically articulated to show his ultimate place not at the centre but at the tragic and fragmented periphery. The death of Krishna Vasudev, mistaken as a beast of the forest, by a hunter's arrow symbolizes this. Besides the grand adventures of the superheroes and the retelling of recycled mythologies mixed with sketchy and invented histories as well as pompous biographies of small-time satraps and boarding-school tutors, the Mahabharata also tells stories of ordinary people, animals and birds ready to sacrifice their happiness or lives for the good of others. Placed against monstrous greed, endless ambition, unbridled lust and resulting devastation, these tales suggest a deeper intent of the poet.

It is here that we come face to face with the originator of Mahabharata. Krishna Dwaipayan Vyas was an adivasi, a fisherman. He was witness to the rapacious progress of urbanization, causing a chasm between man and nature ultimately resulting in chaos. From the rape of nature as a focus, he devised situation after situation at various levels with increasing complexity, providing simultaneously solutions at every stage, either innocuously or cleverly concealed. He raised questions about the equality of man, freedom of choice, women's honour, limits to amassing wealth or attaining power, relations between races and religions. His answer to most of the problems was simple but efficacious—Love. Since changing destiny is not within man's power, suffering will remain a necessary condition of life. But one can always love. Love will hold life. Repeated at countless places are the definitions of a good man. He does not kill. He feels no enmity. He cares for the sufferings of others. Only after his guests, children and servants have eaten does he take his first morsel.

In the clamour of wars and amidst the cacophony of pedagogues, these words are not always clearly heard. But interpolations and editing over centuries have not been able to silence them either. And no one has been able to add anything more to the tragic vision of the adivasi who honoured womanhood, human dignity, animal life, leaves, flowers, dew, springs, rivers, oceans, snowclad mountains, fistfuls of earth and yet cried from the top of the clouds:

'I have been shouting with raised arms, retain your dharma (read love) intact and you will get all you want, but alas, nobody listens to me!'

The time has come, dear Krishna Dwaipayan Vyas, that we must listen to you. We are ready.

This is what this play is about.

Let us start.

DILEEP JHAVERI
Thane, 2005

A Breath of Vyas
(*Vyasochchhvas*)

Translated from the original Gujarati by
KAMAL SANYAL

Characters

Phalguni, Draupadi, Uttara
Dharmesh, Yudhishthir, Duryodhan
Pawan, Bhim, Khandav Van
Vijay, Arjun, Karna
Ashwin, Nakul, Eklavya
Joshi, Sahadev, Ashwatthama
Karsan
Kanu
Kanaiyalal
Kanji Sheth

Act One

Scene 1

Draupadi, Yudhisthir, Bhim, Arjun, Nakul, Sahadev—all dressed in simple everyday clothes.

DRAUPADI. Only because some day a few hundred or thousand years hence, some eunuch, applying mascara to his lashes, chewing betel leaf to redden his lips, his oily tresses flowing down his shoulders, stands on stage, beating his hands wildly, screaming shrilly, 'Oh save me, save me!' as some fatso strips him of his clothes while the audience watches in stunned silence—only for this reason, for this play—you let my reputation be dragged through the dust?

YUDHISTHIR. Duru, I understand your pain. I also acknowledge your wrath. But these words do not become a king's daughter, nor are they in keeping with the noble tradition of our family.

DRAUPADI. I am furious because I am a king's daughter. Because I am the shield of your family, my blood boils with rage. All you cowards just stared at my blood. I came as a bride into this family of worthless louts. Came like a daughter. How could I know that these impotents called themselves Rajputs! Cowards! Eunuchs! Gamblers! (*Continues glaring at Yudhishthir.*)

BHIM. Panchi! Enough! Watch out if you insult Mota-bhai anymore.

DRAUPADI. Oh! So? What can you do? The strength of an elephant in your hands, is it not? Go ahead—wring my neck.

BHIM. Don't infuriate me. Or else I'll really . . .

DRAUPADI. Oh! So my brave moustacheless bridegroom does get angry after all? And where was this anger that day? In the land of the elephants—tying bundles of grass?

ARJUN. It was I who restrained bhai.

DRAUPADI (*mimicking*). 'I who restrained bhai.' You, you! You alone are the real good-for-nothing. Tied to mother's apron strings! Drew your arrow and got alms in your beggar's bowl. 'Distribute amongst the five of you equally!' It's been a tradition anyway in this house to have no less than five husbands.

NAKUL. Di! Enough, I say Mota-bhai! How can you tolerate mother being insulted like this?

YUDHISHTHIR. Duru! Think and be discreet before you speak. Why are you vilifying mother in a matter that is only our affair?

DRAUPADI. Mother? She is my mother too. If I did not have her support, much more than what my own mother gave me, I would have committed suicide long ago. But remember, Ma was fortunate. Her husband would have chopped off the hand of any person who dared point a finger at her reputation. None of you is worthy enough to be even his shadow. And I? In spite of having not one but five—five husbands, I became a widow. What crime did I commit? (*In a soft and emotional voice*) I have cared for and treated you all equally, like the five fingers on my hand. I have been like a maid to all five—all five of you. And at your beck and call. I have not let any one feel neglected. It has been such drudgery since I came here. (*Composed*) Arre, had I married a coachman's son, I might have been cleaning horsedung in the stable but at least I would have been happy.

NAKUL. Di! Even these days will pass. One dark night does not tarnish the moon's beauty.

ARJUN. Krishna-a! Just think. Had we lost the war, we would have been dead by now. We may have lost everything in gambling, but at least we are alive.

DRAUPADI. Arre, what is the meaning of this life where you cannot forget anything? Dark night comes only once a month.

But when my blood spills for days every month, each pore of my body is ablaze. Far worse is the shooting pain in my chest than the pain in my belly which ties me up in knots. Red-hot flames burn in my eyes. Even as I close them, all those black faces float before me. This pack of ghosts will be dancing around me, every day of every month for the next thirteen years. I am waiting for the day when I will see them—in the blood that has oozed from my body—bewildered, and facing a loathsome death. Till then, I will not let my heart stop throbbing! Like this—just as I am now, burning, hammered with every beat of my heart—I will become so sharp that I will cut them all off!

YUDHISHTHIR. Duru! In spite of your rage, you will always remain like a golden lily. I am the offender, and it is you all who are suffering. Even in this, God may have some deep design.

BHIM. Panchi! You will be able to digest this rage like some bitter medicine. Even before you are aware, these thirteen years will pass and with the help of Arjun, Nakul and Sahadev, I shall finish off those scoundrels and elevate Mota-bhai to a stature even higher than now. I will show them. I will kill them all like animals. Crush Dushasan's ribs and drink his blood. Let the world treat me like a rabid wolf and kick me out. I will break Duryodhan's legs and see that he hobbles around with a begging bowl, beseeching death. I will drag each and every son of that blind man into the impenetrable darkness of death.

ARJUN. Bhai! You too get excited, just like Krishna. It is absolutely certain that we will win. But without giving up our dharma, like true kshatriyas.

DRAUPADI. Viju! Let Bhim talk. Dharma and kshatriya will come later. First and foremost is the self. This sick self. A self which has no dharma, no lineage. Which only has a great passion to be alive. Whoever comes in the way of life, has to be totally destroyed. Or else nothing will survive.

BHIM. I shall not spare anyone now. I spend nights without sleep. How often I crawl about in the air. How often I imagine that I hear the cries of my enemies as if they are being strangled and I laugh at the wind passing through the trees. I shout, I yell, I run from this side to that and then how often I sit with my head resting on my knees, staring into the darkness without closing my eyes. Mota-bhai too is unable to sleep. The whole night he sits by me, stroking my shouldes, caressing my head.

YUDHISHTHIR. But remember, Bhim, even these days will pass. Even if we are kicked by fate almost all the time. If not today, tomorrow dharma will certainly triumph.

SAHADEV. Who knows about tomorrow?

Scene 2

The lights change, same place. Vyas-sir, Phalguni/Draupadi, Dharmesh/Yudhishthir, Pawan/Bhim, Vijay/Arjun, Ashwin/Nakul, Joshi/Sahadev and Karsan, the peon.

VYAS-SIR. First class! Not a single mistake today. Each one acted perfectly. A-1. Therefore let's enjoy a cuppa. Ey Karsan! Go, go and get Kanaiyalal's great tea. Eight cups.

KARSAN. Vyas-special, no?

VYAS-SIR. Yes. The queen of all teas.

DHARMESH. No sugar for me.

PHALGUNI. Just seven. I'll have coffee. Nescafé.

KARSAN. Oh that! Kanaiyyo himself, without my telling, with his own hand mixes it. For you.

JOSHI. Vyas-sir! I have a complaint.

VYAS-SIR. Speak up, child. What's on your mind?

JOSHI. I have just one line of dialogue?

VYAS-SIR. Then, has Nakul a lengthy dialogue?

JOSHI. So have we come from an orphanage? Sir! This is gross injustice!

VYAS-SIR. Look Joshi! Justice is always blind. And only the real orphans are given an opportunity to complain. Arre, in spite of having not one but five husbands, Draupadi is forever without a husband. After all she is a barren woman. You know that? When Sri Krishna arrives in the forest to meet the Pandavas, Arjun, his devotee, eulogizes him—says he is omniscient, omnipresent, omnipotent. And Sri Krishna is remorseful that he could not stop the gambling game. During the days of the Rajsuya,[1] he was in Indraprastha[2] for a very long time. And taking advantage of his absence, the king of Saubhanagar, the demon Shalva, invaded Dwarka.[3] Shalva was a friend of Jarasandha—otherwise known as hacker-cracker-and-crusher Jarasandha. Pradyumna, Sri Krishna's son, put up a stiff resistance. But Shalva, humiliating Dwarka, went away. On his return, Sri Krishna found Dwarka in shambles and went off to fight him. But by then the die had already been cast in Hastinapur.

VIJAY. So Sri Krishna never came to save Draupadi from humiliation?

VYAS-SIR. No sir! And that printing mistake was made good after hundreds of years in the *Bhagwat*.[4] You all have an impression of the *Bhagwat*. The scene of Sri Krishna's fight with Shalva is simply fantastic. Saubhanagar was a space city moving in the skies. The whole battle was fought with rockets, missiles, anti-missiles, laser beams, computer illusions—a superb technological fantasy. Arre, if I get a rich and generous producer, I can produce a film that will challenge *Star Wars*. Alas! It's only a dream, like hoping for a water-nymph in a fisherman's net!

JOSHI. But sir! Were there really airplanes, televisions and atom bombs in those days?

VYAS-SIR. What do you think, child? The question is not whether they existed or not. Arre, this is a poet's imagination. A man's heart has no right to beat if watching a bird fly, he does not yearn to scan the skies. And if the word uttered by a poet does not cross the boundaries of time and become the truth, then the sun and the moon and the stars above have no right to rule the universe. Therefore, instead of thinking about whether it was there or not, give the poet the right to imagine.

Give the bard his due sovereignty over his bravado and bagpipes!

DHARMESH. Sir, often the mind becomes giddy. A man can do so much just to keep alive. Just to win he can completely destroy himself. He can build and create a variety of things for tomorrow and then, within a minute, death can turn everything to nought.

ASHWIN. While for some others their undying sick life can become an infinity of misery.

VYAS-SIR. Well, maybe at such a moment, when she found herself totally alone, helpless, with Sri Krishna in front of her repeatedly giving excuses as to why he could not stop the gambling, Draupadi speaks out, 'Not my husbands nor my sons not even you Govind . . . !' Just imagine, when a helpless woman is not rendered help even by God Himself! Her pain congeals and explodes like a supernova. Sri Krishna, singed by this explosion, takes all of them towards the frightful and terrible fire of the great war.

VIJAY. And on the very first day of the war, like the damp wick of a gun, a maudlin and sloppy Arjun presents himself.

PAWAN. But behind Arjun's reservation, sir, wasn't there his love for humanity?

DHARMESH. There is great doubt if he was all that sensitive.

PHALGUNI. I understand only one thing. If a man's life has any meaning, there is only one and that is love. If you get nothing else but love, you can still exist. Love heals everything. Love holds all.

VYAS-SIR. Love holds—that is why love is dharma. It holds hence it is dharma.

DHARMESH. It sounds to me like a moral, a lesson written on the blackboard in school or a 'thought for today' in the middle page of a newspaper. Cliché.

VYAS-SIR. No, n—no. Friend, the last scene of this play brings out the truth of these words. Just like those men who dive deep into the ocean to bring up pearls from its dark bed. The truth adorns the glittering luminous peak of the Himalayas. Dharmesh, just as one has to depend on the words of one's dialogues while acting, in life too a time comes when a man has to depend on his inner voice.

KARASAN. Saheb, here's your tea. And if you have time, big boss upstairs wants to see you. Here's the Nescafé.

VYAS-SIR. Vasudev-saheb must have come up with a new theory once again for the play. This is getting more and more difficult. If you agree, you get your hand chopped off. If you don't—then your nose. And sometimes he has such a brainwave that you think, '*Wah wah*, what a brilliant idea! What inspiration!'

PAWAN. That the play should begin with soliloquies by the dramatis personae was his suggestion, wasn't it?

VYAS-SIR. True. Sometimes one wonders. He is after all a student of science. And burdened with so much work. Meetings at the university, the bother of textbook revision, the chaos in the laboratory and of course, the ever-increasing research papers. In spite of all that, he has a genuine interest in the minute details of our work. Sometimes one even gets bored by his talk. But one has to keep a smiling face in front of the Principal-saheb. So I think it will be a while before I get back. You go ahead with rehearsing the monologues in the first act. Pawan, you can have my tea. The kettle of Vrindavan-brand tea laced with ginger and tulsi must be boiling in Vasudev-saheb's office. (*Exit.*)

JOSHI. I cannot understand Vyas-sir at times. At times he seems quite logical, at times very sensitive, like a poet. On one hand he keeps his self-respect and dignity, but again, he always toes Vasudev-saheb's line. On one hand he is a genius—what enormous knowledge he has! Then again he is happy with inanities, banal aphorisms.

DHARMESH. Manufacturing defect! Congenital disease! He is not free of childhood sanskars. Crisis of identity. After all an OBC[5] seaman. A fisherman.

PHALGUNI. You always have easy answers for every problem. You carry the key to every complex issue. Dharmesh means a storehouse of wisdom. Dharmesh, if you can understand everything, don't you get bored?

DHARMESH. I didn't get bored with you. But you're right. After understanding you . . . (*Takes glasses off and blows on them before wiping.*)

PHALGUNI. Now you're bored with me, aren't you? Happy? But remember, the aversion is equal on both sides. The animosity I feel is so strong—I feel I could drink your blood.

ASHWIN. Hee-hee-hee! Hold on. We have gathered to do a play. The artists must keep aside their personal feelings and perform.

JOSHI. And as Vyas-sir says, only someone who is bankrupt of all originality will go out in the streets and auction his private emotions openly. At the end it all vanishes in the wind.

PAWAN. Child! But what we are performing is not a play—it is life.

JOSHI. What after all is this world if not a stage? Everyone plays a role, plays it well or plays it badly . . . Wait for me! I'm coming. Oh queen of my life and death—my Juliet!

ASHWIN. Once more, once more, once more! Everyone! Standing ovation to the grandmaster of windy platitudes, great rishi Joshi! Phoo—oo!

DHARMESH. But Joshi! The line that the world is a stage is not in *Romeo and Juliet* but in *Merchant of Venice.* In our world, the heart is just a commodity to be traded, just a lump of flesh. Isn't that so, Phalguni?

VIJAY. I feel we should end this topic right here right now, Dharmesh! We all know the history of your relationship with Phalguni and I have forgotten it. The chapter is over. The book is closed. Accounts clear. Phalguni is mine. In May there will be a proper legal registration of the marriage. Do come.

PAWAN. Vijay, you better go to your mother for her blessing only after you have the certificate in your hand or else it better not be—'divide between the five of you . . .'

PHALGUNI. Fatso! I shall smack you so hard one day that you won't forget it all your life.

PAWAN. Hai darling! I am ready to become Keechak just to get a spanking from you.

VIJAY. So then, elder brother, after our marriage it is best that you manage our kitchen right from the beginning.

JOSHI. And then Arjun will be with Sairandhree in the harem for twenty-four hours. Razzle-dazzle all the way.

PAWAN. I have an idea. On the wedding night Vijay will tie strings of flowers to his wrists, light incense sticks, dim the lights and then call his beloved in a soft musical voice. And the bride, sitting in front of the mirror, brushing her hair, will snarl back, 'What are you up to? For the past half hour I've been telling you, have I not, that just give me two minutes. I'm coming.' And then thoroughly fed up, the lover will cuddle a pillow and instead of a bedsheet, cover himself with a sari and fall asleep to the snores of Brihannala. The window curtains and Krishna's hair will fly in the air.

JOSHI. Which means you'll be there walking about stealthily in their bedroom?

PAWAN. Yes, sir. My name is Pawan. To fly about is my job. Happy honeymoon!

ASHWIN. Just think! Everyone must have said 'Happy honeymoon' to Draupadi five times!

JOSHI. And to Sri Krishna, sixteen thousand one hundred and eight times! By the end of it, the suhaag raat would have turned into a sunny morning.

DHARMESH. Where did we begin and see where we have landed? The great Mahabharata to start with and this garrulity at the end?

JOSHI. Isn't there any garrulity in the Mahabharata?

ASHWIN. Sublime and grotesque, noble and base, eternal and transitory, hideous and beautiful, sorrowful and cruel, heroic and cowardly, defeat and victory, victory and defeat—that is the Mahabharata. Full of contradictions. A duel. The Mahabharata of yesterday is the story of our lives today.

PAWAN. And we make the Mahabharata out of each and every trivial moment.

JOSHI. So let us begin. Let each one of us tell his story!

Darkness. Curtain.

Act Two

Scene One

JOSHI (*from behind the curtain*). Honoured spectators, gentlemen and ladies, dear friends! We present here today the first act of a play by Professor Vyas, Professor of History, Jambudwip University. . . . (*Curtain begins to rise*) Oy brother, not yet! (*Faltering in mid-air, the curtain begins to drop*). So then, we present a play written by Professor Vyas, adapted by Vyas, dialogues by Vyas, edited by Vyas—the first scene of the play—*A Breath of Vyas.*

A dusty village. Huts made of grass and mud are scattered here and there. The first rays of the sun are softly caressing the thorns on the thor and baval trees. In the trough sickly cattle, stomping their hooves, are struggling to stand up on their creaking joints. Shaking their heads, goats with short horns and shrunken ribs are jumping, pulling at their tethers. A cock from afar stretches his wings and makes the stray hens picking grain and worms rush helter-skelter. The kabar birds make incessant noise and the crows caw a racket. Suddenly a dog, trying to stop the din, begins to bark. A dog, man's loyal friend. A dog, a companion till the very end. The one who wakes a man from his sleep and also warns of the terminal sleep. Guides a blind man day and night. But right now, barking continuously.

The curtain rises. This is Eklavya's village. Ashwin is Eklavya. In the beginning, Eklavya is squatting, throwing stones at the invisible dog. He stands up as he talks. Moves about the stage. He has a piece of cloth tied round his head, his chest is bare. He wears a dhoti which reaches only to his knees.

EKLAVYA. Bark as much as you like—to your heart's content. I have no thumb now. So there! When I had my thumb I'd made a royal dog dumb with my arrows of dry twigs. Without seeing it. And without injuring it. Why should one let blood flow for no reason? If a respected man who believes that the very sight of us would pollute him gets annoyed at us in our dirty and soiled clothes—can we object? And a dog after all has the habit of barking and pissing. Each one has the characteristics of his lineage. And your karma is what your lineage is.

Mukhio—headman—my father. Instead of just a cloth around his head he'd wear a proper turban to show that his son was different from other Bhil children. He said, 'Learn, son, learn.' But who would want to be guru to a bhil's son? Once I went to Guru Drona and begged him. But he flatly refused. My bad luck. From afar I could see what the king's sons were learning from him. All kinds of things. How to wield a sword, how to throw arrows, how to swing a club, how to ride a horse, how to use spears. We bhils—where can we go riding horses? Our god of trees and animals, Mahadev, hanging on the neck of the snow-white bullock Nandi, will be going about making the sun-moon-stars and constellations go round and round in the skies with his one finger. He feeds the entire universe. And we, who need only a morsel of food and a tumbler full of tadi, who do we have to fight with? Why do we need a club, a sword or spears? It's only when a rabbit hides behind thorny shrubs or a deer disappears behind the trees in the forest, that one needs to know how to kill at one go and with one arrow. To quench hunger. That's good enough. Guru Drona said no to my face but the guru made of mud and dung is dumb. How will he refuse? After all, this body is also a lump of the same soil. When dead, this body is going to be one with the earth. So then I made a clay figure and started practising hitting targets. Even when no one trains, does not a chick born blind fly? A baby deer, born weak and looking like a clod, within no time frisks about, doesn't it? A small stream of water not knowing any direction, turns into a river and meets the sea, doesn't it? The moment Father Sun calls out, all the flowers instantly open their colourful eyes and start spreading their fragrance don't they? Arre, a mango stone buried deep down in a pit for as long as five years blossoms into a mango tree and bears fruit. The nectar of love you give to your wife when you take her in your arms, after nine months, makes the whole village sit up with its infant cries. And to the tune of a flute with five knobs, this earth under the sky, for the past lakhs and crores of years, spins round and round like a top. Is that not a fact? But then, only to show my reverence to Guru Drona, and to keep the sanctity of the vow I had taken, I sculpted him in mud. The blessings of Mother Earth were fruitful. Not just arrows of dried-up branches but of green ones too never missed their target.

We who roam in the jungle, what do we lack? If you walk to where the stone of your sling has landed, you can secure food for the day. If you are in the mood, go and stand in waist-deep water like a crane and you can cleverly catch a boomla or bangda fish. The day you catch ravas, you can invite neighbours for a meal. And to catch partridge and quail, all you have to do is scatter a few seeds and then it's no more than play to kill them. If four men bring a wild boar some day, it's a day of feasting for the whole village. The aroma of brewed mahua flowers or fermented jaggery, its sweetness strained, transforms itself into fire—spreads to your legs, fingers, temple, nostrils, eyes—oh! How it dances! Every night in sleep a life ends and at dawn, a new one begins. And even if it does not? We all have to die. After all, one goes from one home to another. It was only a few days ago. Lakhi, the old woman of our village. Actually she was quite robust. Along with her five sons she had gone to town to some important person's home. They were celebrating some puja or festival. The old lady went to help, cleaning the utensils and sweeping the floors, other chores. The house of the generous hostess, a widow, was made of bamboo, jute and grass. Plastered with gum and sap from our own grove. In the night Lakhi ate with gusto, drank till she couldn't anymore, and went to sleep. Before morning her ship had anchored in Mahadev's dockyard. She had reached home in her sleep—burnt alive. Not alone. All her five healthy sons were next to her. Some die after prolonged illness. Some die with their bones broken. This death was better. Was it not? They say the owners of the house disappeared through an underground passage. But the village? We observed the twelfth and thirteenth day of Lakhi's death. She died but she saved some lives. That punya—is it any less? And those who survived will one day repay the debt, I'm sure. Mahadev will even the score. Who are we to settle the account in a hurry? That's why I say, dog, why should I shut you up if you are able to get a few pieces of bread? Keep quiet. And now listen to what happened once.

I was going through my training in front of my mud guru when a dangerous dog, as huge as an elephant, came barking from that big village. Before your eyes could twinkle seven times, I silenced him. Drona and Arjun just couldn't stop gaping. 'Give me, Eklavya!' Passing himself off as my guru he asked for his dakshina—his fees. He asked for my thumb. So I chopped it off and gave it to him. Now what did I lose in doing so? Even if I had really learnt from him, what more could I have achieved? At the most I would have got a job in the court as a coolie to run around with a load on my back. It is better that I remain in my village, untutored and without a thumb. At least I can catch rabbits and chickens! And what prevents me from charging towards a sambar, catching it by its horns, and with the strength of my arms, wringing its neck? And does not one enjoy playing the flute after drinking sweet-and-sour tadi from an earthen pot brought down from the top of a swaying palm after climbing it swiftly? One note of the flute fills all of Nature. Green leaves, beautiful flowers, vast fields, blue mountains, running waters, white clouds, cold drizzle, croaking frogs and pigeons with their swollen necks, peacocks dancing with joy, deer, fairs in the month of Kartik and bonfires in the month of Poush,[6] Holi on the full-moon night and the pink heels of a fair woman as pink as a chanothi, arre a dark bhil lass smiling with teeth white as shell on her dark face enticed Mahadev as white as the snow? He will take care of that man who was afraid of me—a man of high rank for whom I lost my thumb. I, as low as the very earth, and

I had to lose my thumb. Some day the beloved god of the bhils will certainly take care of it all. A small hint from my Mother Gouri and my Guileless One will sit up and go and give a tight slap to that man and hold him in His arms and turn him to ashes, I am sure. And what about us? The dogs will continue to bark. That is their dharma. And this flute of ours with five holes will continue to be played. And that is our dharma.

VIJAY (*from behind the curtain*). Like scattered rags of grass or jute, like a disentangled string of flax, a doll in dirty grimy clothes is sitting in a corner of the steps, twisting the edge of her sari pallav, biting it with her teeth, muttering to herself, laughing without sound, crying without tears. All around her is complete silence. Let's go quietly and listen. Be careful—she must not see us. Oh, but she has spotted you, Uttara has.

When the lights come on, Uttara/Phalguni is on the stage, looking straight ahead at the audience.

UTTARA. Will I ask a question? I've got into the habit of asking questions. Do you know me? Does anyone remember my name? What did I achieve? What was my crime?

Who am I? This is not the kind of question that someone may ask if suddenly woken up from deep sleep. A person who is unable to sleep, but sometimes does manage to, will answer that question. This is such a question.

Who am I? A doll, a doll made of wood, I was just about that age when you play with dolls. And suddenly something happened—like iron hiding behind wood. And the elders started playing hide and seek. Started performing plays, wearing masks. Some gambled. Some stealthily removed utensils and groceries from the kitchen. Some concealed pots of milk and curds. Some shaved off their beards and moustaches, covered their faces with flour, applied kohl to their eyes, quite thick too. Stuffed their blouses with cotton wool, tied anklets to their feet and began to dance.

Earlier, the maid who oiled my hair, used to talk sweetly about sparrows and pigeons and rabbits. Used to bring, secretly, berries and gooseberries, bits and pieces of tamarind, raw mangoes. If sometimes I could not sleep, she spoke of the fairy of sleep and fairy of forest, fairy of water and fairy of moon and patting my head softly, told me of their magical deeds. Later, a beautiful woman with long curly black hair falling loose over her back used to come instead. She would say in a majestic voice, 'Keep your neck straight, lower your head,' and run a comb of sharp teeth through my hair. Earlier I was used to having my hair bound loose with a ribbon or tied in two plaits. And now? She ties my hair in a tight bun. Eyes damp with tears, if I make a sound she puts her finger to her nose, presses her lips with her teeth and sticks in a sharp pin. What fun it used to be to run and climb the stairs, to swing from the banisters or jump from the chairs! And now? She forces me to walk—looking straight ahead, without spilling a drop of water, an indhoni on my head, a water-pot on top of that, my neck held absolutely erect. Forces me to walk in a straight line, step by step.

I used to split my sides laughing at the maids who, running to obey a call, fell down in their haste, used to enjoy blowing on the silky flowers of the simul tree which blew in through the window, used to love gambolling about. But now? They teach me how to laugh noiselessly, my lips pressed tight. To celebrate the weddings of our dolls we used to decorate the tiny houses with little tanmania flowers. We'd separate the doll bridegroom from the bridegroom's party and put a thorn from the bawal tree in each of their hands, like a sword, and make them walk in a line like soldiers. We would paint our tongues red with chanothi seeds, savouring them as if they were laddus made for the wedding feast. Now in words and gestures incomprehensible to me there lurks the fear of red, the fear of something touching you, the fear of a lizard or a centipede or a snake. If you ask, 'why the fear?'—all you get is a hard pinch on your side.

The other maidservants of the house gossiped without any restraint or inhibition. Joked and sang. Brihannala and Sairendhree, in low voices, gestured and whispered in corners, behind pillars or curtains. Brihannala taught us dance. Her complexion was dark and she was huge. Her fat calves would fill me with dread—if I danced a lot perhaps my own calves would grow similar!

Slowly the questions began to start. And without warning, like a bull charging into a herd of peacefully grazing cows, war was upon us with great force. If on the one hand all the adults went to fight, on the other, the shepherds came rushing in, like goats frightened by a tiger, wailing and panicking. We in the andarmahal bolted our doors, drew our curtains. Our hearts pounding, we clung to each other. Who will save us? The same question the shepherds asked! The only answer: Uttar, my brother. Who could hit a mango on the topmost branch with his gilol, mount his horse in a single leap, with one strike of a sword cut an apple in two? But what could he do—all by himself? Steer a chariot or charge with his sword?

Sairandhree heard this. And off she flew like a whirlwind! Just as it drags out a tree from its roots she dragged out Brihannala. She would steer the chariot and Prince Uttar would fight. Now dress up Brihannala in armour. How angrily Brihannala stared at Sairandhree! With shaking hands the armour was tied on top of her ghaghra-choli-and-odhani, all haphazard. When we tried to to put them in order, the hair on Brihannala's body, the corns on her fingers and palms, the well-developed muscles of her upper arms were all noticed with great wonder. But where was the time to ask anything? More than war, we were afraid of the moment.

The sight of my brother striding about impatiently, blowing his whistle, swinging his sword through the air, gave us courage and I said spiritedly, 'Brother! After conquering the Kauravas, killing their leaders, bring me their silk garments. I will make dresses for my doll Panchalika!' Just then Sairandhree yelled, 'Go!' And then brother and Brihannala ran out in a great hurry. We stood there stupefied, by the walls, in the lengthening shadows of evening now turning red. And Sairandhree paced up and down, up and down, in the verandah.

Then the noise that was gathering in volume far away, rushed at us like a hawk through the balcony: 'Victorious, victorious, we are victorious. Victory to Virat! Victory to Uttar! Victory to Arjun!' My heart skipped a beat when I heard Arjun's name. Wasn't he the archer comparable only to the gods? How did he come to our battlefield? Yet just then, his hair dishevelled, the muscles of his arms sending ripples into the air, his chest so wide—peeping out of the armour, the calves of his legs making the earth tremble, his hand held behind his back, hiding something from view, his head bent, a smile adorning his face, his lotus-eyes dancing right up to their reddened ends, clearing his throat but not saying a word and yet asking something directly, there stood Arjun! Right in front of us, in our courtyard. And my face—helpless and turning red and I could do nothing to stop. He stood before me, held his hand out and waved some colourful strips of silk before my face. Just then Sairandhree ran in, all excited. She snatched the strips and crushed them underfoot. My cheeks were ablaze with anger, my nostrils full of fire, tears flowing from my eyes that would not stop and my heart pounding with joy.

At night my mother asked, 'Want to marry Arjun?' All night I experienced a strange, unknown feeling, every pore on my body burning, turning my stomach into a tightly-wound coil. In the morning Bapaji said, 'Uttara! Touch your father-in-law's feet. Your marriage has been arranged with his son.' The maids started dipping their fingers into a bowl, making me taste honey. And for the first time I experienced between my thighs something warm and thick, like honey. Dressed in a red saree, covered with gold ornaments, staring hard at me—my mother-in-law Draupadi.

What was my fault? When I married him I did not even get to see his face. In the night, eyes turned red by the smoke, I saw only a haze. And then when the war began in Kurukshetra,[7] they said, 'Come, come, hurry up' and took me away in a palanquin adorned with flowers. I couldn't see a thing. But I could hear. Sledges hammering the anvils. Hot iron hissing in water, the neighing of horses, shafts being hurled on ground, painful shrieks of mules, braying of camels, trumpeting of elephants. Thud, thud, khat, khat. Dhamm, dhamm dhamm. Parting the tent's curtain, someone entered. Someone emitting a fragrance. Startled, my fluttering pallav extinguished the oil lamp.

After how many days . . . I do not know . . . I regained consciousness. I had lost track of time because of the mahua liquor I had drunk for the first time—given by them. Then they took off all my ornaments, untied my hair, wiped away the kumkum from my forehead, draped me in a white sari and brought me in the midst of all the corpses. 'This is your Abhimanyu.' Oh! This face still like a lotus blooming in the morning! The neck as white as shell! The fragrance of mahua still clinging to his chest! And this red tinge on his palms and chin and sides . . . oh! on each limb . . . isn't it the red of my sindur? Just one night—and you grew so tired that you came here to lie down? Where is your carpet of golden deer-hide? Wake up! You will wake up, won't you? Or are you dreaming of the apsaras in heaven? Do you see me there? How can I be there? I am here and you are there. Everyone is here still. Father Arjun is here and mother-in-law Subhadra is here. Panchali is here. You too are here. Aren't you? Do you know who is there in my womb? It's you. You are tickling me inside even now. Where are you all dragging me? This is my husband. My husband. My Abhimanyu is here. Where am I? Who am I?

I am a wooden doll. There is an iron ball in my womb. Inside it is a blade of grass. The iron wants to grow soft, wants to live. The blade grows sharp, pierces. But what is my offence? I am just an answer. I am born to be an answer. If you have any doubt, listen. Krishna Vasudev's truth is applauded for making my dead son live. And when my Parikshit is bitten by an insect like a leaf of grass, his son Janmejaya burns snakes. Then to stop him . . . through the lips of Vaishampayan, the Mahabharata as created by Krishna Dwaipayan Vyas . . . and there is no end to acclamation for the creator. That is why I am born. I, Uttara, to applaud and acclaim both the Krishnas . . . a wooden doll covered in tatters—a ball of iron and a blade of grass.

Darkness.

DHARMESH (*from behind the curtain*). The horses tied to their pegs in the stables are chewing grass silently, swishing their tails to flick off flies. Pull their necks and rest them on each other. The setting sun peeps in through the windows. On an empty box, amidst the pattern of light and shadows, sits Karna. Thrashing the air with his whip. Dressed in simple everyday clothes, relaxed, he sits there. No one can gauge what is going on in the mind of this middle-aged man who looks like a friendly neighbour.

When the lights come on, removing his hand softly from his eyes Karna/Vijay looks around.

KARNA. I am scared. What will that Karna be like—who will accomplish what is going on in my mind and whom I cherish dearly? I bathe the horses in the stable every day. I trim their manes and brush them. Massage them. Feed them jaggery, sugar, gram, oats with grass. Pick up the dung baskets, go out and throw them on the rubbish heap. Clean the chariot. Wash the wheels. Wipe away the dirty grease stuck to its axis. Oil it again. Beat the yoke with a hammer to test it. With ash and lime, polish the sheets till they shine. Repair the broken straps of the reins. Apply wax to the leather of the whip. Starch the sagging flags, pressing them with hot pots, making them as good as new. And in my mind I imagine that it is I who am riding that chariot. Hardly have I taken the sixteen-foot long rein in my hand and the horses start galloping, leaving even the wind behind. The roads straight or crooked, even or full of ditches, my wheels slide over them all. Trees and hills, far away, come running near and before they are visible, disappear into the distance within the twinkling of an eye. Like a boat lifted by the waves, the wind makes the chariot fly. Mountains and rivers and seas disappear below me in a flash. A thousand, many thousand hands grow from my body. My arrows fly in all the ten directions, piercing the stars, constellations and nebulas in the sky. Indra, the one with a thousand eyes, grows dim in comparison. And my brilliance makes this whole world . . .

My eyes dazzle at my beautiful imagination. When fearfully I open them, I see this wooden horse, this mud wheel. Toys from my childhood. The horse will not run. The wheel will not move. And even if it does, how long before it breaks and becomes one with the earth?

Even so . . . even so . . . even so . . . from where does this desire to conquer everything arise within me? When I try to remember, a flickering darkness from afar encompasses me. I remember the fatigue of the effort to remove it and the frustration of not being able to. The light spreading across my closed eyes and my eyelids clinging to the redness welling up from within. The lips opening easily to grasp the milky nipple and two rough hands holding me very carefully. The smell of horses' sweat and hay on someone's shirt. When I began to understand what was being said, I recognized my parents, Radha and Adhirath. My whole world existed in the stable . . . time ran past neighing along with the swishing of horses' tails and their ears moving to and fro. The tan of their coats, the taut necks and backs. The harsh sound of horseshoes hitting the floor again and again, the froth at their lips as they chewed grass. Their eyes free of the blinkers . . . the warm moistness mingling with their breath. The feeling of helplessness and strength that could not be separated . . . the strength of a man and the helplessness of a mere charioteer's son . . . the two halves of a wheel. The two together could never make it budge.

If some rejected me for not being a noble kshatriya, some others cursed me for not being a brahmin. I am a man, after all, a man like any one of you, with two hands, two legs, two eyes, two ears, one nose, one tongue and one heart.

I went down on my knees, eyes downcast, ears alert, simple innocent words on my tongue, my heart palpitating, 'I beg you to give me knowledge.' And your answer was 'NO!' To a person who lives by weighing his prospects right from birth, your refusal makes your reputation hollow and lame. Does it not?

I had to lie to acquire real knowledge. I've also been cursed that I will not remember what I've learnt when I am about to die. That's all right. At least I won't forget that I am Karna—whoever gave me birth! Each day has a night. The sun sets but that is not the end. The chariot of my life may be disturbed sometimes but as long as the sun shines, the light of my name will not disappear. That is why I continue to give whatever anyone asks for. I say to myself, 'Karna! Give to the brahmins. Give till their bags of many pockets are so full that they burst.' You greedy ones! Take. Take. After all, how much can you? Till such time that I have a name, I am a man and I have life, the offerings will not be exhausted. Along with that, the praise, whether true or false, on the lips of the receivers will also not be exhausted.

Suyodhan gave a regal name and raised to nobility this unknown person. It made up for what he lacked. This became clear to those competing with the son of Radha. There was no flaw in his weapons nor in his proficiency. Arjun's weapons were blunt because he did not have the courage. So what if my scabbards were made of leather because of my low birth? Now with the help of friend Suyodhan my sword edges will remain ever sharp and glittering. He who turns a servant into a friend cannot be called 'Duryodhan.' He will always be Suyodhan. I will never forget his favour. It is from him that I have learnt to give. That I became the rider of the chariot instead of being its charioteer. There is nothing greater than a man who changes the destiny of a person. These pigmies who call people high or low because of their birth, isn't their own lineage sullied right from the beginning? Many a time, the traditions of this family have been broken. The children born to the two widows were, after all, sired by a fisherman. Weren't they? In spite of that, the one born of a maidservant talks of protecting the Rajput reputation, their bravery and chivalry, which is in truth already soiled. And all this in the name of dharma! Those five Pandavas born of two mothers—whose descendents are they, after all? And yet all five are dauntless and strong. And Suyodhan making a hundred—they too are brave, aren't they? The essence of life is within man, not in his lineage, neither in his pedigree. One's pedigree is like a saddle on horseback. The horse runs, whether the saddle changes or is removed. It all depends on the rider. The soul is the horse and desire, the rider.

Often I think—when will the discord in this family end and how? I close my eyes and imagine and what I see is horses galloping without any riders somewhere in the darkness behind my eyes. Galloping without any direction. Bewildered, neighing, colliding. Neighing up a din. Horses, the colour of nightmares. And when everything grows silent, as far as the eyes can see, there are only horses—so many that you cannot count them—convulsing on the ground, vomiting blood, biting the earth, their jaws broken, their necks twisted, their perplexed eyes staring, sighing softly, groaning in pain—horses, horses everywhere.

Startled, abruptly breaking this gory silence, I return to the stable. Whenever I come to this place and sit on this empty box, I feel at home. Horses are my near and dear ones. The stable, my palace. The joys and sorrows of this palace, my glory. How many kings, so prosperous and of such high pedigree, have I subjugated just by a flick of my whip! I have witnessed their true characters stripped of their prestige. I have seen their women, dancing, throwing off their clothes after a drink—be it wine made of grapes, even fermented jaggery. Seen viragos clutching anyone and everyone, shameless harlots singing in the lanes and bylanes. Sorceresses eating the flesh of camels and horses, sucking the lips of over-exhausted mules. Sows abandoning their own litter, prostitutes indulging in debauchery. A blot on the name of mother.

What am I blabbering?

Who is Karna who is saying all this? I am afraid of him.

Who do I want to conquer? Do I want to defeat Arjun? Do I want Indra to surrender to me? Do I want to defeat Krishna Vasudev? Or do I want to conquer this Karna who is shamelessly abusing thus, who puts his mother to shame? Do I conquer myself? Defeat the whole world by controlling this unbridled and impatient horse?

I will not be afraid. Will not be afraid. Will not be afraid. I will not be afraid of any name, any lineage. Nor of any curse. Nor of any arrow. Will not be afraid of this wooden horse, will not be scared of the chariot wheels which break and merge with the earth. Not of oblivion. Not of the ultimate loneliness.

I am Karna. I give. I give to anyone anything he asks for. Even if death were to come as recipient, the last thing left to me as a man—my life—I will be ready to give. Till that day—the sun shines bright, and the cymbals of light tinkle—till that day I will be here to join the sky and the earth. Me. Karna.

Lights all over the stage then fade out.

Interval.

Act 3

Scene One

ASHWIN (*from behind the curtain*). All around me I hear horses neighing. Clatter of wheels . . . chariots speeding . . . the clang of chariots breaking apart. Rattle of swords, clashing and clanking, hitting shields. Maces colliding, flurries of arrows flying in all directions. Ammunition exploding, forts tottering, screams of soldiers burning and blood sizzling, falling on molten metal. Flags smouldering and the wind swishing by. Clouds gathering in the sky and boulders crashing down. Fearful screams echo in the valleys. The roar of death, thunderous, like the tidal waves of a swelling sea.

Now all that has ceased. (*The curtain goes up slowly and the stage is lit up.*)

Moving his hand on the grey-brown trunks of trees again and again, trees without leaves and bark, in a land unnatural, decrepit and ugly, shaking off the dust on his hands, walking, sometimes with long strides sometimes small, suddenly laughing loudly, gnashing his teeth, sometimes hiding behind trees then looking out and instantly drawing his head back, softly raising his palm, his hand, his leg and at last obliquely, bringing his torso out into the open. Bending back, he steps out in front of everyone. This man, tall and slightly bent, shades his eyes with one hand and seems to be looking for someone. How did you meet him in this silent and devastated forest?

Joshi enters as Ashwatthama. He wears a soiled upper garment and a loose dhoti.

ASHWATTHAMA. My ears are pierced with the neighing of horses, the screams of elephants, the incessant wailing of crows. My nose is filled with the foul smell of my own limbs afflicted by leprosy. My eyes, swollen and red, covered with mucus and dripping water, see this forest through a hazy mist. My skin, white and hairless, hanging loose, rotten and burnt at places, is dead to any touch. And my tongue spouts non-stop, an obscene calumny like thick spittle.

My name is Ashwatthama.

Breaking out in laughter at almost anything, making others laugh at almost nothing, tease, mischievous, playful, clown.

I too am Ashwatthama.

Tall, handsome son of the rajguru, the royal teacher, great charioteer, an equal to no less than Arjun in archery and study of other missiles.

I am Ashwatthama.

Dronacharya, the one who knew the hidden meaning of every weapon but was ignorant of the trickery of words, was my father. Using an elephantine lie linked with my name—the weight of which made Yudhishthir's chariot collapse to the ground. But again, using my name as wings, my father reached the heavens.

Ashwatthama—who is he?

One side of his face made stiff by coquetry, the other, with hanging jaws. No one can tell if that is the limit of loud laughter or the beginning of endless lament.

It's me Ashwatthama. Fatherless. How often I was antagonistic to my father but I never could forget him.

What kind of a man was my father? Born a brahmin, he learnt the art of warfare, but does everyone turn out to be a Parasuram? When he was learning, Drupad, Prince of

Panchal, was with him. The bonhomie of gurukul was mistaken as friendship by Drona. He was ignorant of the savoir vivre of royalty. The smile given to please the subjects was considered affection by him. Like a kite soaring high, thinking—here, I have reached the sky—the brahmin was jubilant. That is when the prince performed such a somersault that with his bust fortune, Drona fell under the curse of poverty. Such poverty that if on any occasion—a birthday or a festival—mother gave us milk, the neighbours knew that it was rice flour stirred in water. The dakshina which other brahmins received without even stretching out their hands, the charity of flour and grains and gifts, never came our way. Father wandered in the forest trying to survive with the strength of his two hands . . . desolate and alone, shaking his hands in the air, suffering the disease of revenge that was to last till the end of his life.

Now I too have to wander in the wilderness with that disease. Because an owl killed the crows. That owl is my guru. But Dronacharya, who became everyone's guru, did not understand even at the age of eighty-five that you cannot trust a king. As was King Drupad, so was King Yudhishthir, his son-in-law. Even more wicked was Dhrushtodhyumna, son of Drupad. When my father was annihilating the Pandava army, he went on hurling unbearable insults at him. Like a wounded lion, my father struck out in anger. Then there was an uproar that Bhim had killed Ashwatthama. With his partiality for Arjun as the ace of trumps, father had hidden me in a corner. But I went over to Suyodhan as a knave of cards. What I did not know was that father's life depended on my name. Hearing the unbelievable news of my death he wanted confirmation. And whom did he ask? Yudhishthir, the very incarnation of dharma. Who is Yudhishthir? A king. A king can make you believe that an iceberg in the midst of an ocean is just floating cotton. So how long can it take for a king to turn me, alive and kicking, dead? In the name of a dead elephant, as if I were a contemptible dog? Father gave up his arms and Dhrushtodhyumna took his life. Ammunition was thrown at my body and my strength and valour exploded. I will not let one person go alive . . . not one . . . not one . . .

not one of the enemies will be allowed to go free—be it elephant or human. Be it Krishna Vasudev with his Sudarshan Chakra or an ordinary footsoldier, dagger strapped to his waist. I have this one weapon—the Narayan Astra. If I do not annihilate each and every one—I am not Ashwatthama. I made them put away their weapons. What of Arjun? I made even Krishna Vasudev step down from the chariot. I made them all beg for their lives. A mute plea. The silence so deep that all you heard was the clatter of my armour-clad arms, the hissing of my breath. The father who breathed his last hearing the whispered news of my death, my ceremonial offerings to him, my tarpan, was given by the ringing of bells everywhere proclaiming my greatness. How do I explain this turmoil within me at becoming fatherless? At my age? A man, when he ceases to be a boy and steps into youth, is already prepared for his father's death. When a son's name is added to the father's, his value increases. Similarly, when the father is no longer there, the son's number goes up one and a half times. By taking the life of Drona, whose son I am, you Pandavas remember that henceforth not one son will exist in your family to call you father! I will make you heirless. Annihilate you all. Not even a fraction will remain of your stock. Just a blade of grass will turn your future to ashes.

I know that my life, which destiny is staring at like an owl, will turn into the ululating of the crows. But I am going to make the owl my guru—who in the darkness of night killed the sleeping crows one by one and ate them all.

Guru Brahma Guru Vishnu Gurudevo Maheshwar. Guru Sakshat Ulukeshah Ulukay[8] Namo Namah. (*Playing on a small drum he dances, round and round.*)

Picking crows one by one killed them all, did the owl
black and raven crows he killed, did the owl
killed the crows in the black of night, did the owl
killed the crows all asleep, did the owl
killed the crows with his sharp beak, did the owl
small and tiny crows he killed, did the owl
killed the crows while a-limping, did the owl

killed the crows while a-begging, did the owl
killed the crapping crows, did the owl
killed the pissing crows, did the owl
killed the crows laying eggs, did the owl
killed the crows crying, did the owl.
laughed and laughed and killed the crows, did the owl
again he laughed and killed the crows, did the owl.

And now, however many curses I receive, whatever kind of curses I receive, whether I have a short life or a long one, the role I had to enact in this play—I have performed. All my desires have been fulfilled. So with satiated heart I want to recite a couplet—just two lines—

When the gathering is to one's liking, the goal is meaningless,
Without any desire I shall wander like a stranger, aimless.

Adieu. Meet again.

Lights go off after Ashwatthama's monologue, then come on again. Dharmesh enters as Duryodhan, attired as a king. A scarf is tied round his neck. He holds its two ends—one in each hand,—as though playing a manjira and sings in the Bhavai[9] *style.*

DURYODHAN. Me Duryodhan, sea of poison,
snake in the Kaurav clan,
Heart full of sin and fraud, whose
father's blind in the eye
Cunning and crafty, harlot and trollop
and debauchee are my pals
Black and fradulent deeds of mine
swell the burden of earth

Envious arrogant avaricious
king of tyrants
All the friends on earth
praise him to the sky.

So you think a villain should be like this? Or (*tying the scarf around his waist like a Kathak dancer*) should he be teasing an innocent, beautiful, helpless, unfortunate wench at some Munnibai's brothel?

> My eyes on your beauty, come hither without your veil.
> Defeated are your five men, come warm my left thigh.
> Let me strum on you, my dilruba![10]

Isn't a villain like this?

Or else. Bell-metal plates tinkling, drums playing by the light of tall brass lamps, throwing gigantic shadows on the temple wall, his stance symbolizing a fight with the mace, he moves round the stage (*demonstrating the* Urubhangam[11] mudra *of Kathakali.*)

Or else. A swimming suit in the latest style, spotless, standing in front of his 'hum paanch,' surrounded by his henchmen and his moll, his eyebrows raised, a cigar dangling from his lips and with a deadpan face, rudely telling them, 'Come on warriors! Put down your weapons! Let your arrows, swords and cudgels rest. Beware! Not a step forward. Open your eyes and look behind me. In the hut smeared with sealing wax is your beloved mother. All nicely tied up. The slightest hint from me and my brothers will torch the place. Now no Vidur or Vasudev will be able to save my blessed widow Auntiji. If you want to save your mother's life, then surrender. Mona darling! Give us a peg. And remember, just one spark is enough. Love for your mother will not let you die. And we hundred will not let you live. Come to take revenge on Duryodhan? The gall! Hyenas in the hide of lions! Shame on you!'

Or else. Do you think the villain is the one in the black clothes with a big sindur streak on his forehead, crushing tobacco in the palm of his hand, spitting the words out of the corner of his mouth as he questions his commander-in-chief who has just returned, defeated?

'Arre, oh Surajbaan![12] How many men were there in front of you? Two? Huh? And how many thousand were you? And yet you came back beaten from Viratnagar? What did you think? That I will be happy? Will give you a reward? Just as

Angdesh[13] was given, will give you Bangdesh[14] on lease as a present? Will have damsels apply balms and bandages with their delicate hands? Traitors, ignobles! Don't you know that even the heavens shake if Duryodhan is angry? Even the sun takes permission before setting on the border of Hastinapur? Arre, even the wind takes my order before stirring. Just the mention of my name and crying children in villages as far away as a hundred kos grow silent. Not a soul—human or animal—dare complain of constipation for miles and miles around. An unmarried woman aborts during her secret visit to the mid-wife just at the mention of my name. Arre, a calf in the belly of a buffalo lying crosswise out of obstinacy jumps out and bellows nonstop, proclaiming victory to me. And you cowards got beaten up by an eunuch of a lad yet to sprout a beard? And came back alive? Didn't you find any wells on the way? To drown in? Couldn't find at least a branch of a khijado tree? Not even by mistake should you dare to implore me thus—Brother! I have partaken of your salt. I am eternally loyal. If you do, you will have this cudgel split your bald head . . . ha-ha-haha-ha-ha . . .'

I am a crooked villain who does not fit such petty imaginings. Therefore let your minds go blind and let your deaf ears be wide open. Listen to me, know what kind of person I really am.

I am Duryodhan. The play in which Yudhishthir is hero, I am the villain. Yudhishthir and I, two sides of a worn-out coin. All impressions and values are erased. What remains is the worth of the metal. The worth of an ordinary man. Whether of divinity or royalty, victorious or defeated, conqueror of all the directions or surrendering everywhere, power or bondage, paap or punya, truth or falsehood, self or shadow, word or echo—all have blended into each other. Only through memory can we sustain each other.

When we were young, and Pandu-kaka had died, these five cousins came to live with us. Right from then the collision began. They were clueless about our urban games. But at climbing trees, swimming or archery, they surpassed us. If we brothers, holding each other's hands, timidly climbed a tree and carefully sat on a branch, our legs hanging over the side, immediately Bhim would hold the trunk and shake it with both his hands and we would all fall down. And he would thunder, clapping his hands, 'I am a tornado, a tornado!' If anyone challenged him, he would hit out with his hands and feet, throwing us to the ground, and run away. Though he was very fat, he was faster than the wind. Sometimes on the odd occasion Yudhishthir would restrain him and he would obey. At that instant our hatred for Yudhishthir would be much more than that for Bhim. Arjun, his eyes closed, would throw just one stone and there would fall plenty of ripe fruit. And when we ran to pick some, Bhim snatched them all away. Then Yudhishthir would say, 'Let them be divided amongst all.' He never knew the fun of eating that which is won in a fight nor the joy of snatching away something before it is given.

Our intrigues would continue and father and Bhishma-dada would find fault and check our ways. Father said, 'Poor fatherless children, and how you harass them. Remember, if tomorrow I am dead, the world will harass you exactly the same way. What meaning is there to a blind man's life anyway?' I was always stung by the fact that everyone wanted to be our guardian because our father had no sight. Vidur-kaka would lecture us at the drop of a hat. But the person we really were afraid of was Bhishma-dada. One glimpse of his reddened eyes and we would be so scared, we'd lose control of our bladders. But he'd cool down very soon, make us all sit before him and tell us stories from mythology. Tales of courage and bravery. Give us instructions and guidance appropriate to royal progeny. The dream of becoming like those sovereigns, like those men of extraordinary achievements, was born then.

Dushasan and I would conspire, as though we were going to attack an enemy king. We'd plan how to annihilate the five, as a start, but such childish desires were always unsuccessful. Once with false shows of love, we made Bhim eat poisonous sweets. Taking part in what he thought was fun and games, he went on eating. The sweets ended soon but not his hunger. He digested even the poison! Once while he was asleep we let black snakes loose upon him. The snakes died but he survived. Yudhishthir came to know of it but said nothing. It was

Yuyutsu who told tales, betrayed us, and we were slapped by father's iron-strong hands. Each blow helped to strengthen the animosity against Yudhishthir for all time.

The memories of childhood are alive, exactly as they were.

From mere boys who learnt to use arms from Kripacharya, we turned into princes who acquired the knowledge of weapons from Guru Drona. If Arjun was an archer without an equal, Sahadev's expertise was the sword. Nakul's speciality was horses while Bhim and I became proficient in using the mace. The days of severe tests during our training became days of celebration. Guru never let Bhim and me face each other. But I was certain that whether in play or in reality, some day I would defeat Bhim. Finally the person who challenged Arjun was the son of father's charioteer. In the beginning we did not even know who he was. But Vidur-kaka declared in front of everyone that no man of low birth had a right to compete with the princes. Adhirath came running up and we learnt that the young man was Karna. To bring amusement to the spectacle I held his hand and announced that henceforth Karna was King of Angdesh. Father had appointed me Yuvraj by applying tilak on my forehead and I used that authority—quite a slap on Vidur-kaka's face. He was furious. Not to let other sons of servants come up in life was the dharma of this son of a servant! Arre, a man grows higher or lower by his deeds. Bhishma-dada taught us so. And yet he supported Vidur-kaka. So that the matter did not get out of hand Karna himself stopped me, put his hand on my shoulder. In the evening we came out of the sports arena. The lamps were lit and our shadows loomed against the walls. The fires, I felt then, had also been lit. With the help of a friend like Karna, we could spread all over the world. The theatrical Ashwatthama was also on our side. He seemed clownish and superficial but was starved for love and affection. He was very hardworking. We were Vaishnavas but he was a stout devotee of Mahadev. Dushasan was as though my other half but still an adolescent. Ardour and disdain ran strong in his blood. Karna had the kind of strength which could not be fathomed. Tremendous self-confidence, but also a hesitation. He was so proud he would not tolerate anyone. But he obeyed my word the moment it was spoken. He was possessed of the one and only desire—to beat Arjun. That was perhaps the only flaw in his character. But then, wasn't I too obsessed with Yudhishthir?

To curb the popularity of the Pandavas, I planned to send them to Varanavat. After settling them into the beautiful house, painted with lacquer and gum, one day, quietly, we'd set it on fire. And sure enough that house was burnt. We got the news that Kunti-kaki and the five Pandavas were dead. But I was not sure. The responsibility had been given to Purochan. But he was burnt too. So without any proof how could you know the truth?

Then later the Pandavas came out openly, at the swayamvar of Drupad's daughter, Draupadi. Standing on the scales, looking at the water, Arjun pierced the fish going round and round above. And won Draupadi. And to the great shame of the entire Kurukul, we cousins and other kinsmen, all five brothers married the one Panchali. Their eyes mocking and sneering, our acquaintances and friends would ask us about it. And behind our backs, ridicule us. When father started to rule, the prestige of Shantanukul had been quite low. Under my leadership and with Karna in command, we conquered many countries and extended our empire. And just then Hastinapur had to face this scandal—this disgrace. When the five brothers came to father for his blessings, he thoughtfully gave them their share of the kingdom and separated them. They stayed in Indraprastha and the blot on our name was removed. As my power and authority spread, I forgot not just my obsession with Yudhishthir but even my relationship with him. Their intimacy with their maternal family of Krishna Vasudev increased.

Once Yudhishthir invited us to join the Rajsuya yagna. Father said that just to keep the honour of the family all of us should go. Vidur-kaka actually started strutting about, his chest puffed up, his neck stuck out, like a pigeon. Bhishma-dada's eyes shone bright, his nostrils flared with pride and the redness of his fair cheeks vied with the tilak on his forehead. Only when I saw Vyas-dada, did I see wrinkles of anxiety on his face. So all of us went to Indraprastha. The Pandavas welcomed us with respect and goodwill. Many kings from within the country and outside had come with innumerable valuable gifts. Yudhishthir said to me, 'So much has come in. One has to keep an account of it all. Also see to it that nothing is misplaced or lost. This is a delicate job, a great responsibility. One can trust only family. Who is there to take this responsibility but you? Besides this will be a good opportunity to know the guests. You as the head of our family will welcome them. That will please them and it will be our pride.' On the other hand, Bhim was in charge of giving away some of the most expensive gifts to the innumerable brahmins. Golden tray in hand, he gave out fistsful of diamonds, rubies and pearls to the mendicants before him, all the while wiping the sweat off his forehead, taking care of his hair. He kept winking and smiling at me, pointing out the lines of waiting brahmins with his glance. Whether that was friendship or strategy, I could not tell.

Yudhishthir gave Krishna Vasudev the highest seat at the yagna. We thought that position was to be given to Bhishma-dada. Many maharajas could not tolerate such an honour being given to a yadav from Dwarka. Shishupal voiced their discontent. So Bhishma-dada intervened. Shishupal insulted him in an unbecoming way. Our blood boiled but we also wondered why Dada poked his nose into someone else's problem. The matter grew out of hand. And Krishna Vasudev cut off Shishupal's head right in front of everyone. There was complete silence. Only the sound of the chakra. It seemed as though the moment of total destruction had arrived. Still, the situation was not allowed to deteriorate. The celebration of the Pandavas was ruined. It left a bitter taste in the mouth. It was also established that Krishna Vasudev would always do what he wanted. And if necessary, the Pandavas would go to him for protection. The thread binding us to them was broken.

But like a needle, the nib of my pen with which I wrote down the account of wealth received by Yudhishthir by way of gifts, continued to pierce me. Gold and silver acquired by digging mountains, diamonds and rubies by digging the earth, elephants, horses, cows, pelts of so many tigers, deer and cheetahs, blankets made from the fur of cats and birds, thousands of abducted young virgins now turned into maids. The wealth of Hastinapur was not negligible. But to me Indraprastha's wealth eclipsed all that. I was sure Yudhishthir would not be able to keep all that splendour. He did not have the courage to fight nor the spirit of adventure. But he did have four brave brothers so one could not snatch it all away in a fight.

Suddenly Shakuni-mama came up with an idea: we should invite Yudhishthir to a game of dice. What we may not get by fighting, we may by gambling. But I had my doubts. Would Yudhishthir who talked of wisdom, of dharma, agree to gamble? But he came with his four brothers. And he continued to lose. Not a hair on his body turned when he lost all that wealth, the wealth he had been gifted without any right to it. After that the real gambling began. First he put forward the sons of his stepmother on whom he had no right. He lost. Then he lost Arjun and finally, Bhim. We thought that was the end. But he was in extraordinary high spirits. He then put himself forward.

Me? I would not offer myself even to God, what of the devil. I am my own master. If God has all the power, well, let Him do what He pleases. But I will not give up living the way I want to, right till the end. And now, here, we had the ruler of Indraprastha in our hands. Not just the ruler of Indraprastha but a man who had earned the highest moral values, virtues and righteousness because of his Rajsuya yagna, the son of a god, one of the seniormost of our Kauravkul generation!

Yudhishthir, who carried dharma on his shoulders, his life was in our hands. Fraction of immortality that he was, he was sold by a mortal. What would remain? Then he began adharma.

After losing himself, he offered Draupadi as prize. Fear and terror everywhere. Everyone realized that what was happening was going to change the course of history. The wheel of time had turned. The one who gave away as gifts the virgins he kept as maidservants, his own queen now became our maid.

He did not even realize his moral degradation. Something in Yudhishthir disappeared for ever. Something much more, much bigger than kul, prestige, wealth, heroism, knowledge, his character which held all this together, his dharma. What shame is left for the one who has given up his dharma? In Dushasan's mind and in my mind also, the old enmity and insults once again sprang alive. The bitterness within spewed out. Turning even more unscrupulous and despicable than our imaginations would allow, we insulted Draupadi in an obscene manner. We uttered what should never have been said. We did what should never have been done.

But Yudhishthir kept quiet. His silence took away all the fun. Then our father gave back everything, keeping Draupadi's respect in mind. The helpless woman used as prize became the Pandavas' vehicle for survival. But who could help rescue Yudhishthir's sunken dharma? To test him, he was called to the game once again. He came. Again he lost and was condemned to exile, in the forest for twelve years and another year to be spent incognito.

What do you think Yudhishthir taught the king of Virat? How to gamble! Before the thirteenth year was over they all came out in the open. Using the almanac as an excuse they began useless discussions. Krishna Vasudev came to negotiate. But what he really wanted was war. There was no flaw in our hospitality. But who can prevent someone from finding fault if he wants to? So let us start the war. Throw Krishna Vasudev in prison. But he who was born in prison was God Himself. To frighten me, he revealed his real face. Why should I be afraid? And if he is God, how can He show anything less than the shape of the universe?

I am a sinner, I am wicked, I am guilty, so why don't you do justice? Put your chakra in motion. Slay me the way you killed Shishupal. But the chakra was not put in motion. That was my first victory. To win at gambling was just a game. But this now is the truth. And now, to win, even God will have to come down, face to face like an ordinary man.

Death was hovering overhead ever since Kurukshetra started. It was a miracle to get up and find oneself still alive. But it was no surprise that we went on being defeated. We went on fighting. We did not give up our kshatriya dharma. Never turned our backs. We continued to be defeated.

But each of our setbacks was a great defeat for Yudhishthir. Yudhishthir who restrained Bhim even at play, did not stop a single adharma by his side. I am after all Duryodhan. Even by mistake do not call me Suyodhan. I am the sea of black ink, darkness of deceits, stigma to Kuruvansh. Have I denied these facts? I am what I am. But when I fought, I fought keeping my dharma intact. And the one fighting against me, the very incarnation of righteousness, purity, truthfulness and dharma, carried on his sinful actions. Wasn't that my victory? Both sides of the coin were erased.

All my life I remained a villain. But at the end of the play these resolute, noble, charming heroes had to become deceitful. Is that a small achievement? My end was victory for Yudhishthir, whose essence as Yudhishthir had come to an end long ago. After winning the war, he had to reflect: what did he conquer? What he lost in winning the war was more valuable than victory, kingdom, fame and wealth. Once you have lost your character what remains? So who is the real victor? The one who stands up erect, his chest defiantly held out, looking about him with alert eyes and a smile on his face or the one lying on the ground, his leg broken, groaning in pain but knowing he has killed the character of his enemy and welcoming the death he aspired to, taking a breath of satisfaction at the end of his life, on the bank of Dwaipayan, the defeated and declining villain?

And this is not all. In a war, a kshatriya who does not back out, reaches heaven straightaway. When Yudhishthir, the favourite of the gods, whose life had become unsavoury with every passing day of every passing year, stood at the gates of heaven in his mortal body at the end of his life, who should he see first but me with a smile on my face? Vexed, he said, 'I do not want this heaven where Duryodhan is.' The envy and enmity, the bitterness, the black ink that I had left behind on the earth, Yudhishthir had tied them all up in his bags and brought them right up to heaven. So tell me, who won?

Lights out.

PHALGUNI (*from behind the curtain*). The chatter of birds, the flutter of the wind as it passes from branch to branch, the fragrance of so many unknown flowers. The change of colour when a raw fruit turns ripe, the chik-chik of a squirrel clutching the trunk of a tree, stopping for a while. The sound of rabbits running, the glitter of the antelope's black skin as it scratches against the rough tree trunk, the shrill beat of a carpenter bird sitting right on top of a tree, the crickets chirping in every corner, the sweet-tongued cuckoo sucking the juice of the mango flowers, the parrots, pricking yellow and orange guavas with their red beaks, the peacocks, unfolding their feathers, swinging their crests, tilting their heads to one side, the waterfalls warbling merrily like children let out of school, the sound of frogs, the yawning tigers lying on their backs, stroking their whiskers with their paws after a good meal, the owls flying away with a great flutter of wings at hearing a snake slide away among the dry leaves, the ants marching in rows carrying shining scarlet grains of the fruit of the umbor tree, the monkeys chewing chanothi, the kites swooping down on the waters of the lake, catching fish in their beaks and flying away, the blue lotus swaying on the ripples made by the breeze, fragrant and heavy with the smell of ketaki flowers, the bees dancing around the jasmines and water-lilies from morning till evening, the butterflies, like weightless moments escaped from a toy clock. In everyday life, stumbling, tired and bored, crushed and suffocated, a success or a failure, rich or poor, small or big—all you have is this dream, this dream which will never vanish.

Lights. A stage with a curtain decorated with big colourful flowers, butterflies, trees with large green leaves, birds, animals, and snakes—like in a children's play. Swinging from one end of the stage to the other, going round in a circle once, Pawan, adorned with flowers, sits right in the centre of the stage. The last part of the accusation he speaks standing up.

PAWAN. Khandav Van.[15] I am Khandav Van. My job in this play is to be burnt. My burning down alone will give strength to each word in this play. Your crime is that you have come to watch. So you have to suffer the punishment.

I am a forest like any other. Aval, baval, baheda, khakhara, simla, khijadam kadamb, karen, bakul, jambu, chiku, phanas, sag, sal, devdar—many such trees are my bones. Streams, brooks, rivers, wells, lakes, these are my blood. Sparrows, kabars, pigeons, titars, baters, titodis, parrots, mainas, chandols, chataks, bulbuls, bapaiyyas—my voice. Worms, earthworms, centipedes, boas—my movement. The herds of elephants are my steps. The lion, my leap; the deer, my speed; the leopard, my hunger; the monkeys, my play; the squirrel, my sport; the bear, my clown; the herds of neelgai throwing up dust with their hooves, my rhythmic clapping.

In the dew are my dreams. My words in every leaf and my song in the air. From morning till evening in the sun and shadow I feast. In the star-studded gatherings, the cold breeze makes my nights intoxicating. Emptying their burdens the caravan of clouds move on. For each blade of my green grass, every day is celebration.

If thirsty, grass will drink from earth. If hungry, deer will chew grass. If the stomach is afire, tiger will catch deer. Cranes snatch fish. Snake swallows frog, crocodile will gorge on turtle. If in the mood, monkey will drink fermented juice from ripe fruit. From ant to elephant, all take life and death in their stride equally and enjoy thoroughly each moment of their life. I Khandav Van, full of endless joy. The earth where even the sun's rays could not reach, I have kept covered with leaves, water, animals, birds and fish. I am the queen of all these five. I am the kingdom and I am its honour. (*Stands up.*)

Now someone's eye with uncontrollable lust cuts through me like a saw. Whose avarice has turned into a tornado blowing over me? Whose greed like a hammer is knocking at my door wanting to be the owner? Intoxicated by power who is trying to snatch the shield of this land's reputation?

Krishna! How many more cities covered with gold do you still want to build? You abandoned Gokul—is Vrindavan now a thorn in your flesh? The huts of shepherds, only as high as a human being, are below your dignity so you want instead to erect palaces that touch the sky? And Arjun! For a body the length of five hands, you find the fourteen spheres of the universe not wide enough to lie down in? So far I had the protection of Rain God Indra. To defeat him, you took the help of Fire God Agni and now the two of you have come to burn me down. Very well. I will be burnt. Each leaf will turn to ash. Each branch will turn to coal. My birds and animals will face calamity. Even the steam from my waters will disappear. My serpents will be destroyed. No part of me will remain.

But I will sprout again. My roots will suck the blackness from all the seven underworlds and disgorge the poison of enmity and envy everywhere. My hay will turn to daggers. My screams, into the shrill cries of your entire kul, reverberating forever. Your blood and the tears of your widows will not be enough to cool my ashes. Your sun and moon and stars will be covered. Your unborn progeny will freeze in the womb. The iron that pounds behind your broken ribs will rust. One marble wall after another will crumble, afflicted by leprosy. In the fortresses built to proclaim your fame, moss will grow and not even one pebble will remain. Your valour will be paralysed, your crippled eyes will be blinded, your name without title, master, will turn to dust.

Guided by greed and the strength of your arrogance if you have exposed the imperfections of this earth, so also your reputation will be exposed for what it is. Then, like a coward, you will be left to wipe your eyes, your head hanging in shame. Helpless. And the gilded palaces of those who have suffocated me with fire, will sink into the waters of the sea. Then like a drowning man, your abundant wealth will plummet to the bottom of the ocean. Arre, this wheel and weapon, the sudarshan chakra and gandiv dhanush, are they the rewards for destroying me? Will their power make your dreams pre-eminent? Even their strength will not be enough to stop the robbers from crushing the remnants of your reputation in the middle of the road. Your descendants by blood, for all time to come, will bear the curse like the sting of the Takshak snake. Generation after generation, the curse will go round and round.

You have come on this earth to strip it bare!

I am Khandav Van. In this play, my job is to curse. I am the oracle of the Mahabharata. Listen to me. If at any time, you too burn the forest or even pluck a blade of grass, then the ashes of this Khandav Van will spread through region after region. Ashes, ashes, ashes. Ashes everywhere. The ruins will be buried in ash till the end.

Darkness.

Act Three

Scene One

Behind the curtain, snatches of Draupadi's speech from the beginning of the play can be heard indistinctly: 'It's only for this reason that after hundreds of thousands of years . . . smearing eyes with kajal . . . that is why you had the robbed . . . .' The curtain slowly rises. More light. Phalguni is doing her make-up. Kanu is applying her eyeliner. Kanu is thin, effeminate and coy. He is wearing a pink or mauve kurta, black shining tights and has long hair. Phalguni holds a mirror in her hand.

KANU. What a dialogue! Only for that reason you had me shamed—so that smearing kajal on eyes, reddening lips with betel leaf . . . ! Turn a little that beautiful face of yours to the other side. Oh what a beauty you are Phalguni! *Kya baat hai*! Your curls and looks so full of mischief! *Hai, hai*! If God in heaven looked at you, even His morality would disappear.

PHALGUNI. Kanu, stop it! Stop this juvenile frivolity! Or else this black line will stretch right upto my ear.

KANU. That is why you will be called Krishna. You know when Vijay calls out 'Krishna' his whole face lights up. A garden in full bloom! I say, you love darling Viju with all your heart don't you?

PHALGUNI. Why? You have any doubt?

KANU. No, no. But everything is over between you and Dharmesh isn't it? Or . . . those old memories? A woman gives her heart to someone only once in her life—like in a *filmi* dialogue?

PHALGUNI. That's the difference between a film and a play. In a film, when the scene's shot it's final. Fixed. Cut. A play is life. A mistake made in one show can be rectified in another.

KANU. Dharmesh is quite pleasant though he wears glasses, of course. But he sweats a lot. How could you stand his smell I wonder! Heard he has diabetes. So he's not going to marry.

PHALGUNI. Soiled soiled soiled! You've soiled my dupatta with the black. If I hit your head with this brush?

KANU. Then I'll cry. I'll shout. I'll condemn you as a tyrant across the whole world.

PHALGUNI. I'll stuff the whole world in your mouth. Keep your hands straight and finish the make-up fast. Or else all five of them will be here and complain to Vyas-sir that I'm the one who delays.

KANU (*helping Phalguni put her costume on*). Ok, ok. There is one thing though, Phalguni. Pawan will never harass you. He is kind. But god! How fat he is. *Phir bhi* . . . His girlfriend will have no fear in going around this vast city with him late at night. Now take Ashwin and Joshi. Mother's milk not yet dried on their lips. Really, such a pair! And they cry and scream and pull their hair without any rhyme or reason.

PHALGUNI. But why are you pulling my hair? Slowly, please.

KANU. What tresses you have! *Kho jau unke makhamali andheremey*—I can get lost in their velvety darkness. Where do you want the knot? Top or side?

PHALGUNI. Moron! You've forgotten. My hair hangs loose. It's only to be tied in in the last scene.

KANU. Right ma'am. Let me have a look. In what leisurely hour has God above created you! He has wrenched the smile from moonlit nights and spread it over your lips. Their red colour is like the flame on the sands of the Sahara.

PHALGUNI. But really! When I was born there was a fire in the hospital. Everyone had run out with my half-conscious mother and bloody me wrapped in sheets. My aunt always taunted me that I'd ushered in fire. They were going to name me Jwala.

KANU. You survived only to set others on fire. You are fire, no doubt. The moment Vijay sees you his eyes are aflame. Fiery Phalguni of fiery kesuda flowers, flame of the forest Phalguni! I too adore Vijay. Ey, will you lend me your Vijay for a day?

PHALGUNI. So now you come out in your true colours. (*She takes off her dupatta and puts it on properly.*) Not to worry. I know your nature. So I don't feel afraid to tidy up in front of you. Regarding Vijay, I cannot lend him to anyone even for a moment. He is mine. He will remain mine.

KANU. Then do one thing for me. Somehow convince Vyas-sir and see that I get one chance to go on stage. As a maid to Draupadi, as the decoration on your forehead. Every day I do make-up for so many people. I dress everyone with so much care. They all go up on stage, do their roles and come back with applause. But my hands are empty. At least once I want to look out at the darkness in front where so many people with bated breath are watching your graceful movements. Without saying a word, they are mesmerised by your voice. Without saying 'uh' or 'aha' they are praising you. *Wah wah*, if I get only one chance to see that darkness . . .

Suddenly Kanaiyalal rushes in.

KANAIYALAL. Run. Run. Finished your work or no? Go. Go fast. You have decorated everything or no? So get lost! Go, go or else I shall send you to eternal darkness.

KANU. I'm going, going. Why the hell are you bullying so much Kanaiyalal? I'll go to your hotel Dwarka and eat till my stomach bursts. And the bill I'll send to you. In return, my love to you, *chikne.* And I'll also have Nescafé till I've emptied the tin. *Tapori saala.* (*Exit.*)

KANAIYALAL. Is it true that you're going to marry Vijay?

PHALGUNI. Yes, But who're you to ask?

KANAIYALAL. Who am I? Can you or anyone else in this world ever understand in this lifetime who I am?

PHALGUNI. What have you to do with my life?

KANAIYALAL. Arre, you are a dolled-up puppet! It's only you with whom I have to do everything. I loved you from the moment I set eyes on you. Remember? That first picnic in college? Sitting on a bicycle without holding the handlebars, Vijay had punctured the balloon you were holding with his air gun? You screamed. Who do you think came running and stopped you from falling?

PHALGUNI. If a balloon bursts suddenly and the coloured water in it sprays on her dress, any girl will scream. Then as she laughs, loses her balance and someone comes and holds her hand, that is love and romance—whoever gave you that idea?

KANAIYALAL. The purpose of love is to hold hands.

PHALGUNI. How queer! So then Dharmesh held Vijay's hand as he was falling off the cycle—what about that?

KANAIYALAL. How does that man with glasses enter this scene? Actually it is Dharmesh who always muscled in. Senior he was, so everyone's big brother. Didn't he stick to you? I had to leave college after first year so my game was over.

PHALGUNI. So you think love's a game?

KANAIYALAL. Not just love, this very life is a game. Listen to my life story. There's still time for the rehearsal. Give me five minutes.

PHALGUNI. Ok, tell. If someone wants to dispose of his life in five minutes, how can anyone deny him the time?

KANAIYALAL. You know I had to leave college because of my father. Just a day before the exams he had an attack of paralysis. You know why? My father, a milkman, running Gokul Dairy, had the ambition that his son—a milkman's son—should receive education and be a saheb. He stopped me going door-to-door delivering milk and made me join Sandipan classes. But my mama violently resented the fact that we should get a good reputation in society. His musclemen started putting salt in our milk cans. Sometimes live cockroaches. We lost customers and unable to face the tension, father had a stroke.

He had to be kept in hospital, tied to his cot. But I didn't let mama go scot-free. Garage-owners from my gang put sugar in the diesel of all the four tempos of his Mathura Dugdhalaya.[16] Engines down. Refrigerator mechanics in my hockey team damaged the coil of their compressor overnight. Their business slumped. Mama had even given out a *supari* in my name. That was an open secret. So I went to Kalia's gambling den as a fake customer. Lifting milk cans, my hands are pretty strong. I settled the matter and the man ran away to his village along with his women. I pawned my mother's bangles, made my mama beg pardon. And acquired Mathura Dairy. And see, in just two years along with the two dairies, I've bought Hotel Dwarka. I didn't even look at you all these days. But every day, my friends brought me every detail of your sweet affair with Dharmesh. I knew though that wise Dharmesh was a loser. Now this Vijay. Since when has he jostled in?

PHALGUNI. Ey mister! Who are you to call anyone a jostler?

KANAI. Baby! You don't know and neither does anybody else. But what I am going to tell you now, don't tell anyone. After Vijay's father died, they were almost starving. His mother used to tie rakhi to my father. That was quite an accomplishment for a simple milkman. Today I have everything. I've even bought a mill behind the hotel in the burnt colony—Khanduwadi.[17] So that someone or the other who always comes from the village with just a gamchha or dhoti can earn a living working there. And whatever profit I make there, I quietly reach it to Kanta-bua. So my mill is the security for your Vijay. With its support he is able to study. Roam round carefree. He is not aware of my kindness. I do not consider it kindness. Once a word is given what is so great about keeping it? The wheel in any case turns on and on. Some pots on it break, some last. The person turning the wheel has no motive. But in case Vijay flies too high it won't take me long to cut the string. So now, say it. Will you be mine?

PHALGUNI. No. No. No. Never! What have I to do with the kindness you have shown to Vijay?

KANAIYALAL. Again charity? Arre, Phalguni Panchal I shall show you real charity when I make you my maharani, I want to build a hotel far bigger than Hotel Dwarka. Hotel Paradise! Five star! It'll take mortals beyond the stars. From its terrace touching the sky you'll see no sign of buildings and slums. Nor the forests or prickly shrubs. Only the gathering of the stars, you, me and divine music!

PHALGUNI. It's a dream, mister, just a dream! Keep it to yourself! What of a hut, I'll even go and live in the jungle with Vijay. Bye. It's time for rehearsal. Thanks for the Nescafé. It'll last a long time the amount you gave.

KANAIYALAL. So you don't want to believe me? All right then. You are rejecting my love as if it's an empty cup of Nescafé. But remember—during the climax of your play, the *vastraharan*[18] scene, I'll come onstage, tearing apart the curtain. I'll put everyone's lights out. Ruin everything. Wrap you in the curtain and run away. Set fire to it all.

PHALGUNI. Excuse me! Oh god of all gods! Don't resort to such madness. And if you really love me, then listen to this. I too am ready to tie a rakhi on you like Kanta-ji or mummy-ji. Swear by milk. That's also a kind of love, isn't it?

KANAIYALAL (*dejected, sits down*). Phalguni, it's difficult to say anything now, I swear. But I don't promise you anything.

Attired in a long-sleeved white safari suit, gold-frame spectacles and shiny white slippers, Kanji Sheth knocks at the door and waits to enter.

KANJI SHETH. Kanaiyalal, you left college because of your respect and love for your father. What has made you come here after so many years? Is your vanvas finish? What new avatar is this? A play within a play! Hair dishevelled, eyes red, flushed face—so wipe the sweat (*Holds out a white napkin like a kerchief*). What thoughts are being churned up? How is Nandubhai's health? What discussion were you having?

KANAIYALAL. Ramayan of Gita Kanji Sheth.

KANJI SHETH. You have not lost the habit of making jokes. Or are you really going to have a relation with Sri Bhagwatbhai's daughter? The selection is quite suitable. Really praiseworthy. But when I got out of the car I saw Dasharathbhai's eldest son, your friend, waiting for you at the gate of your hotel. You were going to promise something? Isn't it? Or is it the case of keeping mum?

KANAIYALAL. I'm going Kanji Sheth. Ciao! I know you don't like me. But we are the future generation holding tomorrow in our hands.

KANJI SHETH. Shake hands then (*holds out his hand*). Bye. *Awajo*[19] bhai. (*Kanaiyalal folds both his hands on his chest and leaves.*) What is wrong with this generation? Century after century the civilization of this country has been based on shanti, sanyam, satyam, shivam, sundaram. Always. Peace, self-control, truth, beauty and prosperity. And now this stylish shocking fashion is shamelessly exhibited. What kind of dress that Kanaiya's wearing! Tight jeans, shirt without buttons and leather waistcoat! How many animals have to be killed for the luxury and comfort of one person! To cover your skin, you peel off the skin of some innocent animal! When will people of the world improve?

Break, explode, destroy, burn! In today's world if you try and teach someone the sense of responsibility you will get such a lecture in return that you yourself will feel ashamed.

PHALGUNI. Kaka, this will go on. No point in taking these people seriously.

KANJI SHETH. How good it sounds when you call me kaka! I too was once your age. But in our youth we had learnt to respect elders. And today's youngsters now call even me by my name. It is the Kaliyug[20] you know. And wait and see. One day, this son of Nandubhai milkman will turn Dwarka into a liquor bar.

PHALGUNI. Generation gap, kaka. The winds of time continue to change.

Enter Pawan.

PAWAN. Pay my obeisance sir! The wind seems to be favourable to us today or what! How are you doing Phalguni-bai?

KANJI SHETH. Everything is fine, son! I just dropped by to see how all of you are preparing. You're putting in so much work so I thought let me go and show my appreciation.

PAWAN. We are fortunate! Sir, tell me, what will you have? Tea, coffee or something cold?

KANJI SHETH. It is really sufficient that you have asked. Actually I do not drink anything but milk. Besides today being Friday, it's a fasting day for me.

PAWAN. Jai Santoshi Ma! Phalguni, Vyas-sir will be late. He is in Vasudev-saheb's office. *Wah*! You are absolutely ready for today's grand rehearsal.

PHALGUNI. But I am already feeling frightened. I'm scared, just like before an exam.

PAWAN. But why? There's more than a week until the show.

KANJI SHETH. Son, in life every day there is an exam and every day there is a show. One should never lose self-confidence. Never. What is there to worry when the one with a thousand hands is blessing you? He is the one who is testing you. And he is the one who gives you strength.

For your show tomorrow, he must have made preparations yesterday itself. All you have to do is work hard. If you work with courage you are sure to be successful and triumphant. Forget about victory and defeat. Do not think about the applause and the *wah wahs. Karmanyevadhikaraste*[21] . . . The show must go on.

Enter Dharmesh.

DHARMESH. Hi Pawan! Hello Phalguni! Arre, kaka! How are you?

KANJI SHETH. Here is success. This Dharmesh made the name of our college shine bright. Gold medallist in B.Com! He proves, if you are brave enough to be a man, God helps you. Success, sweet success.

PAWAN. Sir. He doesn't take sugar. (*Looking at Phalguni*) He obtained something knowingly. What the heart received the hands gave away. Oh brave man! Coming from the gym, right?

DHARMESH. Why?

PAWAN. King Dharmesh! Take a shower after you exercise. And spray something on. As it is, we know you're coming even though you're miles away. Your zodiac sign is Pisces isn't it? No, no. No offence. Just asking.

PHALGUNI. How mean you are Pawan!

DHARMESH. Let him speak. Explode. But Pawan, don't forget that we five Pandavas are the descendants of Yojangandha. The fisherwoman whose smell spread for leagues around her.

PAWAN. For once, Dharmesh, you're wrong. Only Duryodhan and his hundred brothers are the descendants of the fisherman. Hundred per cent. But the Pandavas are the offsprings of God. Correct yourself, check if you must.

DHARMESH. Touché! Fatso wins!

KANJI SHETH. I couldn't follow you. Maybe it's a secret in your play. But Dharmesh! These days I see you in the share market. What do you do there?

DHARMESH. After my B.Com I wanted to learn something about the business so I sit in my uncle's office—Ambika Prasad and Sons.

PAWAN. Sir! You have seen him in the share bazar only recently. But he goes to the race bazar every day. Dharmesh Gandhi, the Sagittarian. The great gambler. He has even taken on an agency to sell lottery tickets.

KANJI SHETH. Dharmesh! Is this true?

PHALGUNI. Kaka, this Pawan is a real fat mouth. You can never trust him. Can anyone depend on hot air?

PAWAN. Beg your pardon, sir! This goes on. Helpless before habits. (*Looking at Dharmesh*) Isn't that true Mahatma Gandhi?

KANJI SHETH. Thank god! Or else I'd have to speak to Ambika Prasad-ji. I know him rather well. Made him the president of the businessmens' association. Isn't he going to have an eye operation?

Ashwin and Joshi enter together.

ASHWIN. Whose operation? (*Seeing Kanji Sheth*) Namaste sir.

JOSHI. Namaste sir!

KANJI SHETH. This pair's always together. Both strapping and sprightly. Science students and fond of the stage. What plans do you have for the future? Both of you are going to be doctors. Am I right? Surgical specialists!

JOSHI. Ashwin's job to use the scalpel. I'm going to be a psychiatrist.

PAWAN. Joshi'll follow his revered father step by step. He'll arrange horoscopes though only for men. But his astrology will not foretell any futures.

KANJI SHETH. There you go, talking about the future and your Vyas-sir has arrived. Come, come, you took a long time.

VYAS-SIR. What to do, Sheth? Being a Vyas one has to go in circles. There can be no inkling of time. So? Have you met my characters? How do you find them?

KANJI SHETH. Arre, can there be anything to say when you have created something?

VYAS-SIR. No no, Sheth. You are their creator. They are moulded by your college.

KANJI SHETH. No, no. The college belongs to Vasudev-saheb. I am only the managing trustee.

VYAS-SIR. Arre, Sheth. What difference is there between you and him? For us you two are one and the same.

KANJI SHETH. That of course is true. It becomes easier to work if men have similar points of view. But now difficult days are ahead. There is a shortage of finance to run the college. Shortage everywhere. Shortage of income to keep alive, shortage of foreign exchange to run the country. Shortage of the earth's resources for man to survive. Shortage of time to sustain life. Shortage of faith for the survival of dharma. Funds have been spent, the treasury is empty. No donations. How can we pay the staff? The burden on the college has increased. Drastic steps will have to be taken. We have to retrench staff. Retire teachers who are unable to control students. Close down departments. Vyas-saheb, how many students really curious for knowledge are left in your history class? I'm just asking. Don't you worry. God's mercy and the government's reservation policy will see that you're not touched.

VYAS-SIR. For that, we adivasis are thankful. Otherwise, any moment, taking paper and pen, in the lap of a jungle or in the fold of a boat by the bank of a river I am ready to write plays. I shall be able to get a bite of bread or a draught of water without anyone's favour. Open air and in the company of a ghazal—what more does a penniless poet need?

KANJI SHETH. So poet laureate! We want to hear your shairi once. Let's arrange a programme of your poetry.

ALL TOGETHER. Yes sir, yes sir, you've never recited a poem for us.

VYAS-SIR. So now listen to the Ramayan that's going to start. Our play is in trouble.

KANJI SHETH. No, no. I have no objection. There was this talk of a stripping scene. So I was a bit anxious. I only insist that you should keep the dignity of our college. No. It is a request. These days the kind of obscene pictures they show on TV-video-cable, the coming generation will be ruined. No such thing should happen in our college. With these good wishes I have come here on behalf of all committee members.

VYAS-SIR. Have you finished, Sheth? You have no reason to be anxious. No one's clothes are going to be stripped off in the play. We want to keep safe even the skin of a deer. Now I have a request to make to you. This city of ours, our country, our earth, slowly but surely are looking obscene without flowers and leaves, trees and jungles, birds and beasts, rivers and lakes. Is your committee going to do anything about that? Right now, we have a small problem—that is about this play. So children! The news is not good. Vasudev-saheb is very keen and insists that we show the war in the play. If not, he won't give his permission. I may keep my personal feelings aside, but how do we solve the practical difficulties? How can the script be changed at the last moment? Where do we get the new characters from? Is a drop of ink going to make Ambika and Ambalika pregnant? And how do I teach anyone to fight? How many rehearsals of war will have to take place? Where will I get the sets from? Where is the time? And where is the money?

KANJI SHETH. I am there, am I not? Why do you worry Masterji? As long as I am there like a maternal uncle with bounties to bestow, you will get whatever you want. You do trust me, don't you? I am with you. I am your servant. Not for nothing they call me Kanji Sheth. Once I give my word, that's it. I shall never break my promise. I shall shake Mount Govardhan[22] just to keep the reputation of a devotee intact. Now listen. TV, video, computers, cassettes have made great progress. Make use of all that. Project whatever you require from back-stage. Sound, light and words—use them all to create the final scene. The electronic and computer technicians of my company—all of them will be here tomorrow to obey your orders.

PAWAN. Sir! *Wah wah*! You have turned out to be our guru!

KANJI SHETH. Son, had it not been so, how could this college continue to be run? College after all is symbolic of this world, this universe, isn't it? But with folded hands I make a request. (*To Vyas-sir*) I am not as educated as you and you are the true guruji. But as a person who is a worshipper of humanity I want to make a request: in your play you show the countenance of God—the one that is described in the Gita—with a thousand hands, a thousand eyes, a thousand mouths. *Danshtrakaralani*[23] *cha te mukhani*, sinister-fanged are your mouths. *Jagdish, Jagdadhar. Parabrahma Paramatma.* The omnipresent visage that the Gita describes, the *virat darshan.* You show that.

PAWAN. Sir, no. Not *virat darshan*—omnipresent presence, but *vishwarup darshan*—*brahmand darshan.* Eleventh chapter.

KANJI SHETH. *Virat* has *vishwa* in it and *vishwa* is *virat*, my son.

DHARMESH. Pawan, keep quiet and listen to Vyas-sir. Sir?

VYAS-SIR. Go on Sheth.

KANJI SHETH. So then, what I said was that using the revolutionary techniques you show the infinite in an atom. Truth in a word. The war will be accommodated in that. Destruction will also be accommodated and so will creation. Now I have a personal request. In the company of these young comrades, just for two minutes, I be allowed to do arati—along with this peerless beauty Phalguni ringing the bell—for that which has no beginning and no end, anadi and anant, the great Creator of the universe. Just for two minutes give this insignificant wretched me a chance. Give me the good fortune of offering flowers to this goddess of the arts on behalf of the college committee. Give me a chance of coming up on the stage, only once. Please think this over. Take your time. I am, after all, your servant. Your decision will be accepted by me with my head bent. I am going. We'll meet again. (*Exit.*)

DHARMESH. Vyas-sir?

VYAS-SIR. Yes, friend Dharmesh!

DHARMESH. Do you feel confident?

VYAS-SIR. You tell me. What do you think?

DHARMESH. This is an age-old move. Give with one hand and take with the other.

PAWAN. That is true, sir. He wants to be on the stage. So he comes up with a bribe—our Shethji.

DHARMESH. All this generosity so that he gets the accolades. The iron hand of power cannot remain hidden behind surface politeness.

VYAS-SIR. This has been the way, child, for centuries. Man has been enslaved by the opium of religion. I am glad you have understood his play in no time. Tell me, what do we do now?

ASHWIN. Sir! You love peace so you do not want war. That is why this calamity. But we are with you in this. We understand your mind. We will go to Vasudev-saheb and tell him we do not want to do this play if its message is for war.

PAWAN. And I do not think Kanji Sheth is going to come back. He really was interested in the *vastraharan.* He thought we were gopis. But we just won't come out of water. Won't give any answer. Let him sit on the branch of the kadamba tree and flutter.

DHARMESH. And the way Krishna could not stop Draupadi's *vastraharan,* who is going to stop the snatching of the cloth covering the falsehood and deception present in our play? Both will cool down by tomorrow.

JOSHI. Who knows what is going to happen tomorrow?

VYAS-SIR. Well said, my orphan child! So you remember your one-line dialogue? Let's begin.

DHARMESH. Why so quiet Phalguni?

PHALGUNI. Where is Vijay?

PAWAN. It's destined that he should roam about. He may be in the lap of Chitrangada or involved with Ulupi or by the side of Subhadra.

PHALGUNI. But you're going to meet only Hidimba fatso, remember that! How can this play go on without Vijay? What could have happened? My right eye is fluttering. Oh god! Come Vijay! Come!

Vijay comes in dragging Karsan by his scarf. Karsan trails behind him, beseeching.

VIJAY. The play will be performed. It will. But this Karsan has already performed a bigger play.

VYAS-SIR. What happened Karsan?

KARSAN. Saheb, I am not at fault or I haven't committed any crime. You can ask anyone.

VIJAY (*pushing Karsan forward*). So you were taken to the police station for nothing?

KARSAN. Please listen to me. The police always want to have something for nothing. So the bastards pick on anyone and hold him. Some day you may also be stuffed in.

ASHWIN. Karsan, are you in your senses? How can you say such things in front of Sir?

KARSAN. Why? Isn't Vyas-saheb a human being like me? As far as the cops are concerned, a sahib and a peon are one and the same. They won't spare even their own fathers. If at all they have seen their fathers. Even their mothers wouldn't know who is the father of whom. Dishonest brood!

DHARMESH. Haven't heard Karsan speak so obscenely before. What happened, Vijay?

VIJAY. On my way I saw this maharaja being taken to the police station. So I asked the sub-inspector, '*Kya bat hai*?' He said it was a case of 207. Also *teenso chauda bhi aur teenso do ka bhi ban sakta hai.* I could not understand all those numbers.

DHARMESH. Listen, 207 is disturbance and breach of peace, 314 is a violent clash and 302 is an attempt to murder.

VIJAY. He was dumped in the lock-up. One constable said, 'Give one leaf of a hundred. I can release him right now.' I thought I could easily manage a hundred but if he's not released even after that?

PAWAN. Right. Finished off all the hundred Kauravas. But the Mahabharata wasn't over, was it?

VIJAY. So I went to the station officer. Senior Inspector Brahme was there. I told him frankly that Sakharam was demanding a hundred rupees as bribe. So he called him and gave him a dressing down. Said that this was a case of rioting and the bail was at one thousand five hundred rupees.

PAWAN. Not sixteen thousand one hundred and eight?

PHALGUNI. Will you stop, Pawania? What happened then, Viju?

VIJAY. Where was I to get so much money? So I went to Dwarka and caught hold of Kanaiya and said, 'Brother, get Karsan out.' Then I and the elder son of Dasharathbhai went with notes. And now Karasanbhai Jesubhai Suthar is present here in person. Notorious worker of our renowned college.

VYAS-SIR. Why was Karsan charged with rioting? Haven't seen him even killing a fly in a tea cup. Didn't you show your identity at the station, Karsan? What was your crime?

KARSAN. I can tell you if you all keep quiet and listen. I had gone to the Nar-Narayan temple as usual. I came to know that the priest runs a gambling den. He sells packets to the lame, blind and crippled. The beggars think that there will be a miracle and they'll will become whole and healthy. Besides, the rascal takes a share from the money they get from begging. I was furious. I had a coconut in my hand and I hit his face with it. Threw away his bench. In the house of God, that rascal, gives up all decency and shamelessly carries on! I was alone and he gathered a hundred. The beggars also took his side. Tore my clothes. Some came with sticks. Some picked up bars and planks. Some had barbed wire, some hammer and nails. I had only God's name on my lips. I was trapped in a circle and all around were those wanting to kill me. Then a whistle blew and the havaldar who collected his share of the bribe came and caught me. Tied a rope round my waist and put cuffs on my wrists. Started pulling me with a lathi in hand as big as a mortar. Looked as if he was going to place me in the pestle. I broke out in a sweat and in my mind I started reciting the *Hanuman Chalisa.* I was walking with my eyes closed when this Vijay-bhai came, I opened my eyes. And now I am in front of you.

VYAS-SIR. This is the limit! History repeats itself after two thousand years. The echoes of the doves released in Jerusalem come again and again from Golgotha!

KARSAN. Saheb! I have never been to Golpitha.[24] I am a bal brahmachari, a celibate from a young age.

PHALGUNI. No children or progeny. Neither brothers nor any other siblings. No one to take the ritual bath after your death. That's why you can afford these violent acts. Vain yogi!

KARSAN. You are the only one who has really understood me. I am a yogi but still I have love for you. And Vyas-saheb, with folded hands, I ask of you a favour.

VYAS-SIR. Hmm.

KARSAN. I do overtime every day with you. Many times I think, I never had any education and I have spent my entire life with these children. I have seen even their children come here for studies. I have taken care of them all to the best of my ability. Then it is each one's own fate. But saheb, give me one chance. Tie that long rope round my waist and wrap rags dipped in kerosene and light it. Let me start a fire, even if it's false, in the Lanka[25] of your play. And save Phalguni like Mother Janaki. Let me bring her out and hear people say *wah wah* and clap. That will give me real satisfaction.

PAWAN. Oh Karsan Bhagat, this is a play about the Mahabharata, not the Ramayana.

KARSAN. A play is a play, is it not? It's the same thing.

JOSHI. Same thing! This lord of lords has not the least idea of time.

DHARMESH. But do you understand one thing, Joshi? Everyone is eager to be in this play, to be a part of it. As if they are going to find the true meaning of their life in the play!

VYAS-SIR. It's here that the boundaries between life and drama get erased. Whatever is left unfinished in life is finished in the play. Reality ends in a dream.

JOSHI. But truth is just an illusion and a dream always remains unaccomplished.

VYAS-SIR. That is why the Mahabharata is timeless. Eternal.

THE REST. And we all are ethereal and will disappear in no time. As if we were never there. Like Vyasocchavas. A breath of Vyas.

VYAS-SIR. Let's have a little rest, then we'll meet for the finale.

Curtain.

Act Four

Scene One

A shadowy, frightful forest. Voices echo. Characters in mythological costume.

BHIM. Oh my god! How fierce is this wind! Just one blow and I was thrown upon this red hot sand. Many a huge tree I've uprooted with one stroke. What a medley of black-faced demons have I tossed up in the air and struck down! Arre, hefted numerous black rocks in my grip, hurled them. Spun elephants round and round as if they were toys. And now this whirlwind is blowing me up like a blade of grass. Come, Arjun, give me your hand once again! There doesn't seem to be any strength left in my knees.

SAHADEV. This grass, growing up to my thighs, cuts like a sword. Arre, Nakul, how did your cheeks get bruised? If there was a mirror handy, I could show you.

NAKUL. Arre! These trees! Are these leaves or razors?

DRAUPADI. I never was afraid of fire. I was born with flames covering me. But I cannot stand this hot burning wind. Where have we come? Where is Yudhishthir, the answer to our hundred questions?

ARJUN. Krishna! This is hell. We cannot meet Mota-bhai here amongst the sinners.

NAKUL. What sins have we committed that we should be exasperated by the foul smell of burning flesh? That we should trudge along this bloody mire, our legs sunk upto our calves?

SAHADEV. Who is going to recognize the past which has gone behind the mirror? Nakul!

DRAUPADI. Viju! Save me. See this huge centipede! It won't bite I hope! Oh maa! See this mosquito. How it's sucking blood from my cheek! Blood here! Once again!

SAHADEV. How grotesque and shapeless our shadows seem because of these dancing flames!

ARJUN. Sahadev! These shadows are our sins!

BHIM. For my enemies my shadow itself was terrifying. But I have not sinned.

ARJUN. Brother, is there anyone among us who can put his hand on his heart and say that he has really never sinned? Arre, knowingly or unknowingly, a man since his birth daily commits innumerable sins. For name and fame, for greed and lust, of what he does there can be no record nor account.

BHIM. Your facile talk is such that anyone would think you are a very erudite and thoughtful person. Mota-bhai is not here. But he has left his chattering tail behind. Oh, oh! Is this a beehive? My mouth? This bee is trying so long to stick to it. Expert archer Arjun! Drive this fly away. (*Slaps his own cheek and crushes the fly between his fingers.*)

ARJUN. Bhai, now at least you have understood what I am saying? This insect you killed—that is a sin.

SAHADEV. Friend! Nothing dies here. For only after death comes hell. Now there cannot be anything like sin. Where everything is dark, you cannot call coal black.

NAKUL. Yes, now I understand the sins committed unknowingly. It is not a sin when you kill someone facing him in many a battle. But during our vanvas, when we were forced to stay in the forest, the insults we inflicted on Mota-bhai who was always against war—that was sin.

DRAUPADI. But it was his sin—his defeat at gambling—which made us go into vanvas.

BHIM. Panchi! Mota-bhai lost in gambling because of Shakuni's sins. For that matter, everyone gambles. What is sinful about that? God above also gambles, doesn't he? He throws us all like dice. Rolling down, some figures point towards heaven and some here. When food is in front of you on a plate, can you say which morsel is going to turn into blood and which into flesh? Which will disappear with a belch and which will be life? The numbers on the dice decide the fate of our game. At least I am not unhappy about vanvas. But Mota-bhai's cowardice at not taking revenge on the enemy was his sin. And we are suffering because of that, by being here—in this condition.

ARJUN. To think of someone as enemy is also a sin.

BHIM. Then why did you fight? Why did you kill lakhs, counting them in numbers? You killed Bhishma-dada with the help of Shikhandi. Killed Jayadrath with deception. I could have finished him off long ago for the crime he committed against Panchi. But it's you who interfered. You said, 'It's Mota-bhai's order.' Tell me who killed Karna? Who was sitting apart without any weapons? And when you had put down weapons on the very first day, why did you pick them up again?

ARJUN. Did I say I have not sinned? But this also is true that on the first day I was confused. I was unable to decide whether to fight or not. Because of some deep insight, Mota-bhai said no to war. And I said no without any understanding. It would have been the same had I said yes. But Krishna Vasudev made absolutely clear what was nebulous and showed it. After that everything happened like a dream—flowing easily.

SAHADEV. That is why what you do in dreams is also sin.

NAKUL. Each moment of our lives is dependent on the creator of the universe. And yet the responsibility is ours. It's he who shows us the dreams and when we try and make them come true, he punishes. Our dreams also are not our own.

DRAUPADI. Tell me one thing. Is all this a dream or reality? Where are we?

BHIM. Panchi! Wake up now. This is the reality. Those vultures, bloodthirsty, staring with bent necks and open beaks is reality. Those animal eyes like burning coal, the grinding of their teeth, the scouring of their nails, are real. These red hot pebbles, this river of pus, this stink of excrement, the harsh trill of the crickets, this moss clinging to our hair, these mosquitoes buzzing around us, biting us, these insects crawling all over us, these spiders' webs grazing our breaths—all this is real.

SAHADEV. But we are false. We are illusions. We are the dream of the creator.

DRAUPADI. Then we are also his sin. And his punishment.

SAHADEV. True. True. Along with us, the Creator also is suffering because of His karma. That is why He takes on a new avatar, again and again. Just imagine! He created this universe but it is so full of chaos, that He Himself has to appear time and again. To shape it anew. To make it whole and healthy. Hits it with His hammer here and His toe gets crushed. Another blow there and His palm gets bruised. Something torn and you want to stitch it and you end up with the needle pricking your finger. You go ahead and solder something and your eyes burn. At last, angry, He breaks up all that He has made by hitting out with a sledgehammer.

BHIM. He has always had someone like me to help Him break things.

SAHADEV. What man breaks is trivial but an atom Hari breaks is glorious.

ARJUN. That is true and I understand it now. Krishna Vasudev said many many things to me at Kurukshetra. I forgot. When everything was totally destroyed, he explained again. But I was still confused. Yet my life continued with whatever was won. To win was my life's only meaning. But later I was defeated, so much more badly than Mota-bhai had been. After Krishna Vasudev left, my bow with its arrow that could aim and destroy anything living or dead, became a hollow stick. I was left with a voice cracked and hoarse, a cripple. Just a caretaker. Dwarka, submerged under the sea and orphaned was robbed and plundered. I could not even save whatever little of its prestige was left. The butter that Krishna Vasudev had churned became ghee poured through a sieve.

SAHADEV. Friend! Don't you think God made this earth all right but in a haphazard way. Then He sat down to judge what was good and what was bad. His first remedy was to finish off what was not required.

NAKUL. But it is the last remedy to cut off that limb which is wounded and septic.

BHIM. If you do not sever what is rotten right in the beginning the result will be that nothing healthy will survive. A little rot will turn everything rotten. How many times, we could have just crushed our enemies between our fingers, so easily. But Mota-bhai never agreed. So later crores were massacred. In the beginning there were only a hundred. But later how many more zeroes were added unnecessarily. I believe in straightforward accounts. If someone whom I have not hurt blocks my path, I will not leave him. If my strength happens to be less, I will die. The one who is stronger, will win. And only those who have strength should live.

SAHADEV. All have to die one day.

DRAUPADI. But do all have to rot in this hell? After death?

ARJUN. This question can be answered in two ways. We feel the Creator has been unjust. And that too is a kind of shortcoming on His part. Is it possible that God wants to obtain perfection through us? If we see the fault of the Creator, we are also the ones who give Him the chance to create something new after erasing us. When Krishna Vasudev was relating the Gita to me, there was a lot that was contrary to the other and a lot that was being repeated, over and over again. Like a continuous churning without any plan. Maybe, while explaining to me, he himself was trying to understand. Trying to produce some kind of order from anarchy and chaos. Well, we are created by God. We are rejected by Him. But it is true isn't it, that we were a kind of surprise to Him? We are the people belonging to Kaliyug. Selfish, greedy, self destructive, destructive of all, wicked, sinful. But something must have been lacking in the people of Satyayug, which is why perhaps God wanted to see the result after adding wickedness. We are the descendants of evil. But that evil was created by God. So how can we forget that even here in this hell we are a part of the same God? God is not all powerful. Or perhaps he definitely is not.

But we yearn for God with great ardour. That ardour is everlasting. At the end of his life, man links his grievance with immortality. Can there be a better fortune than that?

BHIM. Here we are, burning, stinking, irritated, how can this be called good fortune?

ARJUN. So now there is the second answer. Where do we come here from? Instead of acting out a play with a tragic end, let us try and find out from within. Were we wrong somewhere some time? Our drawback, our deficiency will become our strength to tolerate this situation. Now let us calculate our sins.

SAHADEV. I have not committed any sin. If just to be a man is sin, then I understand myself as no one else can.

ARJUN. Arrogance of intellect—that is sin.

NAKUL. During the days of vanvas, I had repeatedly drawn Mota-bhai's attention to my looks being ruined by the sun and the chill and there was a lot of distress. That could be the reason.

ARJUN. Pride of beauty—that is sin.

BHIM. I always scolded you. But I am not sorry. Because you were younger than me and also if the bubble in your brain burst, it would make room for some wisdom to grow. That's why I pestered Mota-bhai. That's how he got the opportunity to think with an open mind in the fresh air. The only regret I have is that I tore open wicked Dushasan's chest but did not drink all his blood. I am still thirsty. I am sorry that I did not break the other leg of cunning Duryodhan. The hunger for revenge is as strong as ever. What a mess I made of Keechak. Except for these, no other desires are left to be fulfilled. Had good food, had good things to drink. Enjoyed myself.

Digested uncooked rice as well as poison. This hell to me is like a big burp after a very satisfactory meal.

ARJUN. It's impossible to grasp you, bhai! But this is the sin of gluttony. Now Krishna, your turn.

DRAUPADI. I was always proud of my beauty. Like Nakul. And why not? It was my beauty that fascinated the five of you. And when I was left alone, I had completely given up all of you. And my own children. I had drowned the memories of my father and brothers too. Washed my hands off Keshav Govind Krishna who had gone on a journey when I was being disgraced. At the end who dissipated me was the one who made me survive. But I went on despising him. Condemning him. Dharma, dharme, dharmesari Yudhishthir. And went on loving you more than my own life. You, Viju! I have always been yours. I have loved only you. You and only you—

ARJUN. Sin of partiality! Now let us tally my sins. Along with Narayan, I had taken this avatar, incarnation•of Nar, of a man. And to remove the burden of sins on this earth, I have committed more sins. How many birds and beasts I have hunted to feed the dependants! Burnt down forests, killed men. Just to be called the best among men, I deprived many of their rights. Or conquered them by deceipt or cunning. And even after gaining possession of a person like Draupadi, I made love to many other women. Thinking I was obeying the wishes of Mota-bhai I kept passing off my own responsibilities to him. Many a responsibility I undertook but did not fulfill. To win was dharma. Under the protection of Mota-bhai and Krishna Vasudev I continued performing unpleasant adharma. And yet, I was unable to save my own son Abhimanyu. And I murdered Karna, born of my own mother.

When Mota-bhai showed distrust in my heroism, blinded by my pride, I showed such contempt that it must have been a savage blow to him. The result—I was defeated by Kabha, an ordinary robber. In short, I had all the weaknesses of a human and yet continued to believe that I was the best of men. In the end, like Sahadev, I must say my sin was the sin of being a human.

BHIM. *Wah, wah,* Arjun! What you say is right. Now truly I feel relieved. We have owned up our sins and just see, how the air has changed. Where does this fragrance come from? This sweetness?

DRAUPADI. I know. I know this fragrance. This scented breath. This is Yudhishthir's smell. Yudhishthir is somewhere near us. Where are you? Where? You are there somewhere near are you not? (*Her voice echoes softly.*)

Yudhishthir arrives in a palanquin carried by four angels. The angels are Karsan, Kanaiyalal, Kanji Sheth and Kanu.

YUDHISHTHIR. I am here. But here there are rotting corpses, burning bones, dancing skeletons and echoes of my name. Where is my Draupadi? Where are my brothers? You have carried my burden all the way from heaven . . . What are your names? Kanu, Kanaiyalal, Kanji, Karsan—isn't that so? This palanquin handled by four, carried my life that was as long as only a moment. Life is only just a twinkle in the Creator's eye, no? But a living man can see the end of his life. A long road, an unending road of life—my brothers and Draupadi carried my burden on it and walked on. Like the sky, the fire, the air, the water, the earth—Draupadi and my brothers looked after me, took care of me. And I—I dragged them like a soul dragging a body. My passion and greed, my idiocy, my cold-blooded simplicity, my vacillation, my cowardice, my indecisions, my vapidity—I put the burden of all these on their shoulders and, light as a flower, I indulged myself in finding answers to the profound questions of life. I asked whoever I met. A new guru every day. Even when I received answers I asked the same questions over and over again. Whatever I heard I repeated like a parrot. At the end I learnt the difference between dharma and adharma. Then I tried to follow what I believed was dharma. I blundered, fell on my feet. And realized that dharma need not be victorious always. Then I also believed that where there was victory, there was dharma. I made others believe the same. In the end I understood that no victory is the ultimate victory. I knew dharma but could not preserve it. I bowed down to adharma. Not only that, I even made adharma my partner—believing that later I would once again follow dharma. It is absolutely certain that one has to pay the price for having immoral relations with a whore. I was burning within all my life. If that was not the entire payment, then I will pay what remains by being in these flames, in this darkness. I shall suffer for giving up dharma, to preserve dharma, for not recognizing dharma.

Now I do not need this palanquin. I will search alone for my Bhim, Arjun, Nakul, Sahadev and my beloved Duru whom I won without any effort and whose husband I became—I will find her all by myself. These pebbles and embers will not deter me nor these wild birds and beasts nor this terrible blackness. Unshod and unarmed, only with courage, I will cross all barriers. If you want, be patient. Meet them all. Where are you Bhim—my very breath?

BHIM (*as though from afar, offstage*). Here I am, Mota-bhai.

YUDHISHTHIR. And where is my strength—my Arjun?

ARJUN (*as though from afar, offstage*). Very near you, Mota-bhai!

YUDHISHTHIR. My dearest Nakul! Where are you?

NAKUL (*as though from afar, offstage*). I am here—you can see me can't you?

YUDHISHTHIR. After the first, the second beat of my heart for which I always wait. My Sahadev! Where are you?

SAHADEV (*as though from afar, offstage*). I am or I am not. Now that is the question.

YUDHISHTHIR. And where are you Duru? I am a coward as always. I am the same one whose voice has just broken. Who looks into the mirror again and again and, finding his thick eyebrows joined together, tries to rub furiously at them with his finger, biting his lip in concentration. Who peers at the faint growth of his newly sprouting moustache, pulls at the hair on his chin. Who admires his own biceps after raising his shoulders and straightening his neck. Who wipes the sweat from his armpits. Mother Kunti's obedient son whom you turned into a man called Yudhishthir! Duru, where are you? You will find your lost self within me.

Draupadi comes running, misses a step and falls. Yudhishthir holds her hand and helps her stand.

DRAUPADI. I have found you, I have your hand. I have your support. Now I do not want anything.

YUDHISHTHIR. Duru! Duru! If I had not found you I would have lost everything.

DRAUPADI. And nothing we have lost can be compared to finding you.

One by one the brothers step into the light and meet Yudhishthir.

YUDHISHTHIR. Duru! Are you all right?

DRAUPADI. How do you find me?

YUDHISHTHIR. Tired, defeated, scorched—the way you were during our days of vanvas. Beautiful without a match.

DRAUPADI. Those days you felt I was as delicate as a golden lotus inside. Even though I used to be burning outside, inside I was cool because you were there. Now that you are here, it's cool all around.

BHIM. That is true, bhai! We were owning up our sins and suddenly there was a breeze. The air was full of fragrance. We realized that it was the strength of truth.

ARJUN. But in fact, to tell the truth, it was the strength of your dharma.

NAKUL. Of your good deeds.

SAHADEV. Because of your existence.

DRAUPADI. Shall I explain this relief?

YUDHISHTHIR. Yes.

DRAUPADI. First you tell us what guided you here.

YUDHISHTHIR. If you had asked who then I had an answer. These four. Kanu, Kanaiyalal, Karsan and Kanji. The first letter, ka. But what pulled me here was love. My love for all of you. You were my comrades in my days of happiness and days of sorrow.

Without any fault on your part—how very much I have harassed you. I was the cause of all your sorrow. You were the cause of all my happiness. Holding each other's hands we saw this earth. We saw affluence and power, we saw slavery. We saw fame and we experienced dishonour and disgrace. We saw honour and dignity, saw deceipt. We fought a lot, too, among ourselves. Without coating it with sugar, we expressed the bitter truth to each other. We also accepted that we would never understand each other. But we never gave up our companionship. Our smiles and our tears, our anxieties always stayed linked. The love that existed in defeat, that same love existed in victory.

DRAUPADI. So now you know where that cool fragrance came from? From your two hands it flowed. The fragrance of love.

YUDHISHTHIR. Now we shall always be together here. But tell me one thing, what place is this?

K.K.K.K. Yudhishthir, this is hell.

YUDHISHTHIR. This is your illusion. Where five of my own are there, where love is, there hell can never be. Love is our everything. And if you believe that the place you brought me from is heaven, then go back there. Go Krishna! Go for ever. We shall not say *aawajo*—come again—to you. You preserve your heaven. For us this love is enough.

All six join hands with each other.

Curtain.

Notes

1. Rajsuya yagna: a fire ceremony to establish one king's sovereignty over all other kings.
2. Indraprastha: the capital city constructed by Yudhishthir after he received his share of the Kuru kingdom from Dhritarashtra.
3. Dwarka: rich megapolis founded by Krishna on the western shore of Gujarat after his people migrated from the north.
4. *Bhagwat*: The book dealing with Vishnu's incarnations, centred around Krishna, providing a detailed account of his birth, early childhood and early adulthood. The final version was compiled during the third–fourth century AD.
5. OBC: Other Backward Castes, a governmental category.
6. Kartik is an autumn month usually beginning after the festival of Diwali and Poush is a winter month.
7. Kurukshetra: location of the famous battle between the Pandavas and the Kauravas described in the Mahabharata.
8. Uluk: the owl.
9. Bhavai: a folk-art form of Gujarat, largely farcical.
10. Dilruba: a stringed instrument played with a bow, also meaning the beloved.
11. *Urubhangam mudra*: stance in Kathakali symbolizing the fracturing of the thigh. Bhim had struck Duryodhan's thigh with his mace—an act against the rules of combat—at Kurukshetra. The scene is often enacted in Kathakali and is also the subject of a Sanskrit play.
12. Surajbaan: Literally, 'an arrow of the sun.' A derogatory reference to Karna.
13. Angdesh: a state gifted by Duryodhan to Karna to elevate him from his low caste to royalty.
14. Bangdesh: Bengal.
15. Khandav Van: the forest set ablaze by Krishna Vasudev and Arjun to appease Fire God Agni. The forest was inhabited by the snake tribes and Takshak, a snake who managed to escape, later took revenge by killing Parikshit, Arjun's grandson.
16. Mathura Dughdalaya: reference to Mathura, capital of Kansa, where Krishna Vasudev was born in captivity.
17. Khanduwadi: reference to Khandav Van.
18. *Vastraharan*: the disrobing of Draupadi by Duryodhan in the

royal court. Also the hiding of the clothes of the bathing gopis by adolescent Krishna Vasudev.

19. *Awajo*: The Gujarati form of saying goodbye, actually meaning 'come again.'

20. Kaliyug: the present era of evil, the last of the four ages.

21. *Karmanyevadhikaraste*: a quote from the *Bhagvad Gita* which says that right to action is the only right granted to man.

22. Mount Govardhan: the mountain Krishna Vasudev lifted with his little finger and held over the people of Gokul in the manner of an umbrella, protection against the torrential rain inflicted on them by jealous Rain God Indra.

23. *Danshtrakaralani*: part of a stanza from the eleventh chapter of the Bhagvad Gita describing Krishna revealing his universal form in its frightening entirety to Arjun.

24. Golpitha: a red-light district in Mumbai.

25. Lanka: the kingdom of Ravana in the Ramayana.

A Note on the Characters

ABHIMANYU: son of Arjun and Subhadra, married to Uttara, died at a very young age. Killed by unfair means at Kurukshetra.

ADHIRATH: Low-caste charioteer, foster father to Karna who was abandoned in a casket by his unwed mother Kunti.

AMBALIKA: wife of King Vichitraveerya who died childless. Later, impregnated by Krishna Dwaipayan Vyas to give birth to Pandu.

AMBIKA: elder sister of Ambalika, another wife of King Vichitraveerya; also impregnated by Vyas to become mother of a blind son, Dhritrashtra.

AMBIKA PRASAD: literally, 'the gift from Ambika.' Reference to Dhritarashtra.

ARJUN: son of Kunti, sired by Indra. Kunti was married to Pandu who died childless, cursed to spending a life of celibacy.

ASHWATTHAMA: son of Drona, the teacher of martial arts and warfare to the princes of the Kuru dynasty.

ASHWIN: reference to either of the twin gods Ashwinikumar, physicians of heaven.

BHIM: younger brother of Yudhishthir and second of the five Pandavas.

BHISHMA: elder of the Kuru dynasty who renounced his right to the throne and took a vow of celibacy to procure Satyavati's consent to marry Shantanu, his father.

BRIHANNALA: name assumed by Arjun when he was forced to live as a eunuch due to a curse from the celestial nymph Urvashi, whose advances he had spurned. This turned out to be a useful boon for the mandatory year the Pandavas spent incognito; as an eunuch he taught performing arts to the Virat princesses.

CHITRANGADA: warrior-princess of Manipur who fell in love with Arjun and married him

DASHRATH: father of Ram, an incarnation of Vishnu.

DHARMESH: 'the righteous,' a reference to Yudhishthir.

DHRUSHTODHYUMNA: Draupadi's brother.

DRAUPADI: daughter of King Dhrupad, wife of the five Pandavas, also an incarnation of Lakshmi, consort of Vishnu.

DRUPAD: King of Panchal and fellow- student of Drona.

DUSHASAN: second son of Dhritarashtra. Literally, 'difficult to discipline.'

DWAIPAYAN: middle name of Vyas, literally, 'born on a *dweep* or island.' Also the name of the lake where wounded Duryodhan sought shelter on the last day of the battle of Kurukshetra.

EKLAVYA: bhil prince who was denied entry into Drona's class because he was a tribal.

HIDIMBA: female demon who fell in love with Bhim. Bhim killed her brother and married her.

INDRA: God of rain and thunder, comparable to Zeus.

JANMEJAYA: Arjun's great grandson who started a Sarpa yagna, an elaborate ritual which would result in destroying the entire snake population of the world, to avenge his father Parikshit's death from snakebite. The Mahabharata was recited to him to inform him of his ancestry and to restrain him from the carnage he was planning to unleash.

JARASANDHA: literally, 'joined by Jara.' Enemy of Krishna Vasudev. Father-in-law of Kansa, the maternal uncle of Krishna Vasudev who later killed him. Born in two halves and abandoned soon after his birth, he was joined together in an invincible body by the female demon Jara.

JAYADRATH: Husband of Dushala, daughter of Dhritarashtra. Attempted to abduct Draupadi from the forest but was foiled by Arjun and Bhim who punished him by shaving his head except for five tufts of hair, a reminder of the five Pandavas whose wife he had attempted to dishonour.

JOSHI: astrologer. Reference to Sahadev who was granted the power to foresee the future but was denied its revelation.

KABHA: highway robber who defeated aging Arjun in his vain attempt to protect the women of Krishna Vasudev's clan after his death.

KALA: poisonous snake polluting the waters of the river Yamuna. He was driven out heroically by child Krishna Vasudev.

KANAIYALAL: colloquial for Kanhaiya Lal. Allusion to Krishna Vasudev's romantic aspect.

KANJI SETH: reference to Krishna Vasudev's protector aspect.

KANTA-BUA: 'aunt Kanta.' Reference to Kunti as the sister of Krishna Vasudev's father.

KANU: reference to Krishna Vasudev's playful image.

KARSAN-BHAI: reference to Krishna and Jesubhai, to Jesus.

KARNA: son of unmarried Kunti, sired by the sun god. Abandoned by her and raised by the childless charioteer of the Kauravas, Adhirath, and his wife Radha.

KEECHAK: brother-in-law of the king of Virat intent on molesting Draupadi while she served the queen disguised as Sairandhree during the year the Pandavas spent incognito. Beaten to death by Bhim.

KRIPACHARYA: brother-in-law of Drona and earlier, teacher of the Kuru princes.

KRISHNA: another name for Draupadi, because of her dark complexion.

KUNTI-KAKI: 'aunt Kunti.' As addressed by the sons of Dhritarashtra. Kunti was the wife of their paternal uncle Pandu.

NANDUBHAI: reference to Nanda, foster father of Krishna Vasudev.

NAR-NARAYAN: the two sages Nar and Narayan reborn as Arjun and Krishna Vasudev; also an incarnation of Vishnu.

PANCHI: nickname, short for Panchali, used by Bhim.

PARASHURAM: an incarnation of Vishnu who annihilated the warrior classes several times; also teacher of martial arts to Bhishma and Karna.

PARIKSHIT: son of Abhimanyu and Uttara, a stillborn revived by Krishna Vasudev.

PAWAN: literally, 'the wind.' Allusion to Bhim being the son of the wind god.

PHALGUNI: a constellation. One of the names for Arjun.

PRADYUMNA: son of Krishna Vasudev and Rukmini.

SAIRANDHREE: another name for Draupadi.

SANDIPAN: allusion to Sandipani, a teacher to Krishna Vasudev.

SHIKHANDI: brother of Draupadi, perhaps an eunuch. Reincarnated as Princess Amba of Kashi. Rejected in marriage by Bhishma because of his vow of celibacy she immolated herself and was reborn for a revenge which actually resulted in the battle of Kurukshetra.

SHISHUPAL: powerful king betrothed to Rukmini who was in love with Krishna Vasudev with whom she eloped. Shishupal's existing animosity against Krishna Vasudev was intensified by this act and he never let go of an opportunity to denounce Krishna Vasudev for his lower status among the warrior clans.

SUBHADRA: sister of Krishna Vasudev, married to Arjun after a sham elopement. Mother of Abhimanyu.

SUYODHAN: an alternative name for Duryodhan, literally 'easy to fight with.'

ULUPI: rincess of the Nag (snake) tribe, married to Arjun.

UTTAR: son of the King of Virat, forced to take arms alone against the Kaurav army.

UTTARA: younger sister of Uttar, wife of Abhimanyu.

VIJAY: 'victory.' Another name for Arjun.

VIRAT: the king who sheltered the Pandavas during their year spent incognito.

VISHNU: principal deity in the Hindu pantheon. An evolved form of Indra, hence known as Indra's younger brother.

YOJANGANDHA: literally, 'one who smells for a *yojan* or five miles.' Another name for Satyavati, mother of Krishna Dwaipayan Vyas. Raised by a fisherman and apparently reeked strongly of fish.